Broken Family Bonds:

Poems and Stories
From Victims of Parental Alienation

Broken Family Bonds:

Poems and Stories
from Victims of Parental Alienation

A book of stories and poems written by victims for victims to help them understand and see they are not alone and the pain is real.

PAS Intervention

A federally tax exempt charitable organization approved to accept deductible contributions under Sec. 501(c)(3) of the IRS.

LuLu.com/
Online Self-Publishing

LuLu.com Edition

ISBN: 978-1-304-11318-4

~~~~~~~

This book is dedicated to all the families who suffer from the abuse of Parental Alienation. PAS is a form of domestic violence perpetrated using psychological abuse. The stories and poems are real. The people are real. The hurt and anger are real. Let's not forget this and work to intervene early with prevention and intervention so we can stop PAS from harming any more families.

PAS INTERVENTION

A federally tax exempt charitable organization approved to accept deductible contributions under Sec. 501(c)(3) of the IRS.

Table of Contents

About PAS & Acknowledgements

From the Founder of PAS Intervention, Joan T. Kloth-Zanard:

This book is a labor of love and commitment to ourselves and other victims of PAS to provide a powerful outlet for support, education, advocacy and action.

PAS Intervention and I would like to acknowledge all of the members of our support groups who suffer every day from this form of psychological abuse. Every one of them, who has contributed to this book or helped me with this non-profit, PAS Intervention, has given so much of themselves and opened up in hopes of helping just one more person. A special thanks to Shelley Carlisle who took over this project so I could concentrate on other things, and to Kristen Saffa for coming up with an amazing logo for us.

Parental Alienation is one of the worst forms of psychological abuse. As an alienator tries to destroy one's ex-spouse, the children's and target parent's heart and soul are ripped to the core. In this book are the words of the victims of this type of abuse. Their poems and stories tell of broken hearts, frightened children, the devastation of the parent-child relationship, and more. For many who have contributed to this book, it took all their might to write about the heartache and pain they endure every day; many are numb from the pain. Whatever the reason for their contribution, it is their way to get their story out there and hope they can and are making a difference every day, in someone's life.

~~~~~~~

"If you love until it hurts, there can be no more hurt, only more love."

~ Mother Theresa

~~~~~~~

HHSS

Remember to strive to be HHSS!!!

Happy, Healthy, Successful and Spiritually Positive.

Success is not about money but about where and what we do in our lives.

Spirituality is not about religion but about believing in a positive way about ourselves or something else that has spiritual meaning to us.

PART ONE
FIRST EDITION - 2012

This book began in 2012 with the collection of stories from victims both parents, children, grandparents and extended family. With each year we will include a new part as the next edition of the compilation of horrific stories and emotions stemming from the alienation and estrangement from a once loved child or parent. Please understand that each of these people is pouring their heart and soul onto these pages about what it feels like and what they went through being denied a relationship with the people they love.

Chapter 1

Helplessness
by Amy M.

Helplessness is trying to be a part of a family and it not working

Helplessness is reaching out for help and constantly being told no

Helplessness is trying to love unconditionally but constantly being verbally berated

Helplessness is trying to do what is in the best interest of the children and constantly hitting walls

Helplessness is looking for resolutions and not finding any

Helplessness is reading books, talking to attorneys, meeting people in the same situation as you are and still feeling alone

Helplessness is feeling useless and sad

Helplessness is feeling frustrated and angry

Helplessness is fighting for justice, getting nowhere and wondering if it's all worth it

Helplessness is wondering if the kids "will ever get it" no matter how many years pass

Helplessness is being a victim of Parental Alienation Syndrome

~~~~~~~

Chapter 2

My Second Wife, a Short Story

by Christopher R. E. Zanard

I married my first wife in 1982 and we had one son (1982). We divorced approximately 4 years later. This wife and son I see and speak with and have no issues with. It is my second wife, who I have two children with that has been the source of all of our problems. I married my second wife in 1987. I have a son (1988) and a daughter (1990) with her. She was verbally and emotionally abusive of my first wife's son, whenever I was not around. She actually tried to destroy this son's relationship with my first wife by telling him that his mother was no good and berating her. When this did not work, after my daughter was born, she tried to convince me to go after my first wife for custody of my son. She was told by the agency that unless his mother was abusive or a hardcore substance abuser, she would never loose custody. At this point, the abuse to my eldest son from my first wife apparently got even worse, only my son never told anyone. It put a major riff between myself and my first wife and son for almost 10 years until my present, third wife came along and patched things up.

I was separated for nearly 3 years from my second wife. During those 3 years I had generous and liberal visitation. There was never mention of abuse or claims of DV. After about 3 years of this separation we decided it was time to get a divorce. We agreed to use the same attorney so that we could keep the costs down and make it fast and easy. That is when I went on with my life and began to date my present wife. As soon as my 2nd ex found out, she switched attorneys without notifying me and filed for divorce without properly notifying me. I was not present for the divorce proceedings and the judge did not even think twice about making sure I was properly served or rescheduling court to make sure that I had gotten the

4

notice. The sheriff had served it without any signature and it had been apparently delivered to my landlord's home. By the time, I received it, it was too late, she had been to court, gotten sole custody and awarded an astronomical amount of child support based on her word and not a single document. The judge did however say that visitation was to be general and liberal. Despite this order, my ex impeded repeatedly. She continually refused or impeded with my visitation. I filed a motion for visitation and that is when she filed the false allegations of abuse. It took 8 months to prove that the allegations were false but by that time it was too late, the damage had been done. She had already brainwashed and programmed the children to hate and fear my new family and me.

I tried to go back into court pro-se to have the child support overturned. But despite tax returns and a letter from my physician about my bad back and knees that had put me out of work for quite sometime, the judge refused to reduce my child support. It was not until I was forced to obtain an attorney who used the same tax returns and medical information, that my child support was reduced. My ex refused to accept this and instead tried to have it overturned claiming I was frauding her and the courts. When this matter finally came to the courts, my ex tried to submit a bogus day camp bill for $3600 along with a dental bill. My present wife and attorney proved that the day camp bill was only $500 or $600. The bill she submitted was forged. She had committed perjury, forgery, defamation, and slander and gosh knows what other laws she had broken. The judge was pissed and told her that the only person committing fraud in that court was her. I am fairly sure that she returned home and told the kids that I was a horrible terrible person who lied in court and was not paying her enough child support and gosh knows what else.

As for all the court orders for visitation and counseling, she impeded with those repeatedly. The first court evaluator who concluded that there was no domestic violence based on a lack of evidence and the fact that during our 3 years of separation she allowed me to see my children 2 to 3 times a week, without a single complaint or police report to back up her allegations of abuse. This evaluator went on to say that anything the children knew had been directly told to them by their mother. She also stated that it seems I had gone on with my life and made a lot of positive changes, but that my ex was refusing to accept this and get on with her own life. She recommended counseling for everyone but my ex refused to go, though she would eventually take my children at the most god awful hour of the morning (the children were 6 and 8 at the time) to a therapist that she had convinced I was the problem. This therapist refused to read the evaluators report and only took my ex's word for everything.

A year or so later, another evaluation was done. This evaluator refused to read the original report and at first was swayed into believing the ex's stories. But she did state in her report that the ex was refusing to go on with her life and this time she court ordered counseling. My ex continually impeded with the counseling orders. First she lied and said she changed her medical insurance and the chosen counselor did not accept it. We found out this was a lie, and so her new excuse was that we had seen the counselor before her and tainted her. Then the evaluator found another counselor and this time she really did change her insurance to one that the counselor would not take. Then she claimed that she was not going to force the kids to go to counseling and she did not need any. This is when the evaluator began to finally get it. Though to this day the evaluator has never apologized or changed her report to reflect these issues, it is documented in other ways, because at this point, a court appointed attorney had to be assigned to protect the children's wishes. It was this court appointed attorney who ordered a Guardian Ad Litem to be appointed to protect the children's rights.

The court appointed attorney motioned for the ex to supply her with her medical insurance information and a list of counselors. The ex never provided such a list. We did. We found out that she was on the same insurance as us and so we could provide the list. The CAA court ordered the use of a counselor off of this list. As soon as the ex found out, she immediately changed the kids insurance to one that this counselor did not accept. This would be the 2nd insurance change to prevent counseling. In the meanwhile, the GAL was taking the ex's side and not really doing anything to get things worked out between the kids and I. It would be at least another 3 court orders later before the GAL started to get it. The turning point was when the ex lied to the GAL telling her that our attorney badmouthed the GAL to the judge. The GAL called up our attorney screaming and yelling at him. Our attorney told her to check the transcripts, that none of what she was told had happened. That is when the GAL started to get it.   But at this point, it was some 7 years into the case and the damages were so bad between the children and myself.

Well, despite a 6th and final court order for visitation and counseling, the ex continued to impede. She would do the same things she did when she took the kids to the first counselor years ago. That is, as soon as the children got out of their session with the counselor, she berated and denigrated me and destroyed every bit of progress that was made.

It is now 9 years later and I still have no relationship, not even remotely with my children. The GAL has all but given up as well. The CAA was pulled off the case years ago. And our attorney feels terrible because there really is not much more we can do since the kids are too old.

There are a lot more bits and pieces in between obviously to this story. But these are the basics. My present wife has spent since 1996 studying this form of psychological abuse. She has put together a program for the courts, counselors and agencies that would help to predict, which parents are at a higher risk of impeding the relationships and help prevent and intervene in the high conflict divorce cases. She just does not have the funding/backing to take it to the courts and get them to use it.

~~~~~~~~

Chapter 3

Taken
by Cyndy Rudd

You murdered me without a weapon
Strangled me and no one heard
Picasso'd every dream
And made the "outside" look so absurd

But the voice got louder every day
The one I lost along the way
The one at the core "of who I am"
That nurtured me when you "didn't give a damn"

Afraid to peek behind the mask
Afraid to not do every task
I would give my life for these kids
But cannot pay your ransom

So instead of baking cookies
I wear the scarlet "A"
Though I have no secret lover
I have born all the shame

So well fed on this diet of adversity
That I grew larger than the fear

You took everything but my freedom
So I must also leave my sorrows here..........

~~~~~~~

Chapter 4

Daddies Aren't Supposed to Cry
by Doug Watts

Daddies aren't supposed to cry

They aren't supposed to hurt inside

Or ask the question why

But when his little girl says that she hates him

When she tells the world she would rather replace him

Then he feels the sadness deep inside

That¹s when he wishes he could die

But instead he gets down on his knees

He says Lord, won't you tell me how

How the woman I once loved, can hurt this one love now

She was once my wife, together we made this life

You know I hurt so bad and how this makes me sad

I trust in you and all you do

But I can't take this anymore

She's taking my little girl from me, this one that I adore

His girl says Daddy, why don't you ever call

Why don't you come to my plays, or watch when I play ball

He says baby, I leave messages for you everyday

And I promise, I didn't know about your play

I love you more than anything, and will until my dying day

He says goodbye, then hangs his head to pray

He says Lord, won't you tell me how

How the woman I once loved, can hurt this one love now

She was once my wife, together we made this life

You know I hurt so bad and how this makes me sad

I trust in you and all you do

But I can't take this anymore

She's taking my little girl from me, this one that I adore

She says when I'm 18, I'm going to change my name

You're a poor excuse as a father, in fact you're just plain lame

When I was mean to you it was only because you deserved it

Mom told me the truth, about how you wanted to hurt us

If you really wanted to be with me you could have made it happen

If you really wanted me in your life you should have made it happen

He says Lord, won't you tell me how

How the woman I once loved, can hurt this one love now

She was once my wife, together we made this life

You know I hurt so bad and how this makes me sad

I trust in you and all you do

But I can't take this anymore,

She's taking my little girl from me, this one that I adore

Years later, She decides to re-connect with her dad

She calls him, only to hear he died very sad

He never stopped loving her he said in a letter

He said I'll see you again someday, and it will all be better

She just hung her head to cry

She said I've never done this before, now I'm gonna try

Lord, won't you tell me how

How the Dad I once loved is not here now

My mother, she was his wife, together they made my life

I hurt so bad this makes me sad

I trust in you and all you do

But I can't take this anymore

My Dad has been taken from me, the one I should have adored

A Biographical Short Story

by Doug Watts

I would be in an awful place if it were not for my wonderful wife and 1-year-old daughter.

Regarding my 23-year-old son who changed his last name – we barely talk. I do still get calls from him on my birthday and father's days, he usually attends events with my family once or twice a year (as long as nothing is going on at his mothers). So that is a good thing. He is graduating from University of Tulsa May 5th and he told me he was sending me and my side of the family announcements but we have not seen them yet. I keep inviting him over for dinner, to go up to our lake house, etc but he never accepts.

My 16-year-old daughter has not stayed the night with us since March 6th, 2011. She comes by maybe once or twice a month to see her sister and maybe watch a movie. I try calling her every-other day and if I don't get voicemail she will answer and talk for maybe 2 minutes before telling me she has to go. It is very hard and depressing at times, but I try to stay focused on the positive and extend grace often. It really broke my heart when I didn't get so much as a call on my birthday. My pastor tells me I need to lower my expectation and increase my commitment, and that is just what I am doing here. Last time I spent Thanksgiving with her was 2007, spring break 2007, and Christmas 2008.

We were supposed to have court last week but it was again postponed; this time because the judges husband was having an operation. My original motion to decrease my child support based on a decrease in my income was filed April 2009! Several other motions were filed in 2009, and 2010 to start my visitation back up, enforce visitation, and for contempt on my ex-wife but none have been ruled on. The judge did however increase my visitation back in October by giving me what is now the standard visitation schedule which then cut my child support in half based on the incomes of my ex-wife and me in 2005. Of course, actual visitation has not increased and my attorney asked me if I wanted to file yet another motion to enforce of contempt against my ex wife and I declined, saying there are still at least 4 such motions before the court now that have not been ruled on.

I have had 2 meetings with our judge in her chamber where she admitted seeing the Pluto movie and reading material I gave her. She said that was all for children much younger than my 16 year old daughter. I didn't mention that my daughter was 13 when my motions were filed! LOL! The judge just told me that I needed to keep in contact with my daughter and work on getting her to come around. So that I what I am doing. Even though I really feel like giving up at times.

~~~~~~~

14

Chapter 5

Was, Is, Could Be

by Greg Brede

In my thoughts, I can still see us playing catch, ice skating, skiing, tire swing, loosing your first tooth, watching Disney Videos, laughing and having fun. You were 6, 8 13 and 16 at the time. This one-way view into what was still brings a smile to my face, calm throughout by inner self and a yearning to reclaim what was once the center of my life. These precious memories can still be cherished by both of us, as we still exist. These precious memories cannot be cherished as the result of circumstance that others have succeeded in.

I can still remember the challenges that I had with your other parent that also loved you very much, but we did not get along for quite some time. To no fault of yours, we argued, disagreed and brought out the worst in each other. I loved you enough and make a choice to shield you from this and your mom and dad no longer are married; but we are still your mom and dad and love you very much.

I can vision that someday we will once again have a parent child relationship. It will be different than it was now six years ago. When we get the change to talk of when we played, skated and skied is may be twenty years from that time; but at least it will be in our lifetime. Neither one of us is gone; only apart. I look forward to making amends to what others have taken from us. When you grow and realize what was taken from you and hear what I have to say, I have high hopes that your will understand.

Until then, know that you are loved, you are a good kid and I am proud of you.

~Your Other Parent

Chapter 6

Perpetual Youth
by Jetika Zanard

Asher B. Durand (1796-1886)☐Landscape, n.d. Oil on canvas

It was kindergarten, maybe the start of first grade, when my stepbrother and sister and I found the giant rock in my back yard. It was hidden in the woods covered with leaves. It was the perfect rock for a fort.

For days and days we cleared out all the leaves, pretending that deep inside the huge crack of the rock lived a family of snakes, so we had to be careful and not walk on the crack. We found brooms and rakes, and worked hours on end as if we were professional landscapers working hard on the job.

When the rock was finally cleared of leaves, it was time to collect the sticks. My brother wanted huge, long sticks, he had a plan. We must have found at least thirty of the biggest sticks I could carry at that time. I had no idea what my brother was going to do with them; all I knew was that it was going to be great.

For days and days he strategically set up the sticks, leaning each one against the rock so that they began to form a circle. As he worked on his project my sister and I began examining the secrets hidden within our new fort. The rock was slightly separated in one part, with a crack the perfect size for me to sit on without falling through.

My brother handed me an extra stick and told me to do what I'd like with it. My sister and I sat in the crack holding the stick trying to find the perfect thing to do with it, when she began singing, "row, row, row, your boat, gently down the stream..." as she moved the stick around pretending to paddle a boat.

Since that day, every time we went to the fort we pretended to get into the canoe and row into a land of unknown. About a week went by when my brother finally finished his masterpiece, he had made the greatest, most spectacular tepee I'd ever seen. It fit each of us inside perfectly, if we went one at a time.

After the tepee, the fort really began to take shape. We found an old rope in my dad's workshop and an unused piece of wood, which soon became the impossibly dangerous swing. It started with rope, yellow as the sun, one side tied around a tree and the other side connected to the rock.

Then came the wood, rectangular, no more than a foot or two long, and no wider than maybe six inches. We attached it to the rope, I can't even remember how, all I remember was it was completely unstable. My brother got the hang of it pretty quick, he was able to balance on the wood and swing back and forth ever so slightly, while my sister and I fell backwards tumbling down the little hill of leaves, dirt and rocks, every time. Eventually, my sister and I gave up on the swing, and stuck with our "canoe."

The fort was fun, and we had put so much work into it, but

there was so much more to be found within those woods. So one day, we took a walk, which was when we found the tree. The tree that had fallen in between two trees and was perfectly horizontal between them. My brother of course, the monkey he was back then, climbed it immediately, showing just how great he was being able to get up there and walk around.

I was only six or seven at the time, but I had guts, and I wasn't too far behind him climbing up to that tree. My favorite part of the tree-fort was the dangling vine. It hung from a tree way up, and looked just like a vine that Tarzan would swing from. We used to hang onto it, swinging back and forth, pretending to be in the jungle, with all the elephants and gorillas, just like Tarzan.

Back then; Tarzan was my dad's favorite thing to watch, so we had all the necessary background to figure out just how Tarzan would swing on this vine. Every time my stepbrother and sister would come over we'd play in the woods, running back and forth between our two forts that we had so perfectly put together.

However, time had begun to pass and I began seeing them less and less. The tree-fort was cut down, along with the Tarzan vine. A little while later, a few storms had past and the tepee had past with them. Sometimes I still go out into the woods, just to sit on top that rock that brings back so many good memories.

Memories that prove, "In the woods is perpetual youth." If I close my eyes, I can see us sitting in the crack pretending to row the boat, and hear us singing as if we were sailing across the Atlantic. I can see the vine swinging from the tree, with my brother holding on for dear life calling out sounds only Tarzan would be able to understand. I remember having the most difficult time climbing up that rock, that now takes me no more than two seconds to climb.

The tepee is there, in pieces, no longer standing, but the

sticks lay silently, reminding you of its presence. Reminding me of the time I spent that summer, the last summer, I saw my stepbrother and sister.

Angels are forever!

By Jetika Zanard (age 7)

Dear Jerry,
I am very sorry for what has happened to you. There might have been a reason for you passing away. But I think there was no reason for you to. I think you should have lived if not much longer than at least longer than you did! I also don't just feel bad for you I also feel bad for your Mother and Father because they are probably very very sad because of what has happened. Mommy has always told me very good and funny things about you. She tried to find you once a year, but no one knew where you were. I have missed you very much but now I will miss you much more because I will never see you except in pictures. Now that you are gone, the angels are by your side and watching over you.
LOVE YOUR
DAUGHTER, JETIKA!!

Chapter 7

Unbroken Bonds
by Jennifer Weber

Your daddy's love for you is a bond not to be broken

It is innocent and pure without a need to be spoken

The precious time he has is never time enough

And missing all your "firsts" makes things more than rough

To be separated once was an utter vile shame

To have it happen twice; we understand this is no game

For reasons known to God and only God Himself we must endure this test

We pray your father's tenderness shines through, putting all this misery to rest

~~~~~~~

Chapter 8

The Power of Healing Through Our Words and Actions

by Joan T. Kloth-Zanard

Every time we tell our story, we heal a little more.

Every time we help someone else out, we heal a little more.

Every time we send a prayer, we heal a little more.

Every time we say something good or nice, we heal a little more.

Every time we reach out and touch someone, we heal a little more

Every time we remember to love ourselves, we heal a little more.

Every time is starting to add up and will heal us every time.

Current Biography

for Joan T. Kloth-Zanard

My husband, Chris Zanard, still has not seen his kids since 2006 and they still will not speak with him. We cannot do anything about that as they are too old now, but we do know that their mother stills hammers away at them about their father and her hatred and anger for him. This makes it impossible for his kids to ever get a break from her. It is for this reason that I continue to run and volunteer with my 2 Free Online Yahoo Support groups and provide free counseling as well as have established a 501(c)(3) Non-profit to help victims of PAS. The first six chapters of my book "Where Did I Go Wrong, How Did I Miss the Signs?" are available on the www.pas-intervention.com website.

Hope

by Emily Dickinson, submitted by Joan T. Kloth-Zanard

Hope is the thing with feathers

That perches in the soul,

And sings the tune--without the words,

And never stops at all,

And sweetest in the gale is heard;

And sore must be the storm

That could abash the little bird

That kept so many warm.

I've heard it in the chillest land,

And on the strangest sea;

Yet, never, in extremity,

It asked a crumb of me.

Conversations with Patience
Analogies of the suffering of our children as seen by the targeted parent

by Joan T. Kloth-Zanard

So I was thinking the other day about some comments made pertaining to how we are told to have patience when it comes to our children coming around, especially when they are very young and vulnerable. Basically, we were discussing how we are always told to just be patient. Well, to me this is like knowing that another country has an atomic bomb that they are going to use, and being told to be patient about not stopping them from setting it off. These alienators are like atomic bombs waiting to go off. Do you sit there and just watch and wait to see if they are going to set it off, or are you going to do something about it to prevent this world war from happening? Just seems like common sense to go in and try to prevent what is going on, instead of just sitting back and waiting.

The point is that all the courts and professionals keep telling us to be patient and that the kids will come around. But that is like waiting for a country with an atomic bomb to come around and decide what to do. Do you sit there and wait for the bomb to go off, or do you get proactive and prevent the bomb from going off. Same idea. Why are we being □told to sit back and wait for this atomic bomb to go off, when we could be doing □things to prevent it from happening.

Misti:

What is so difficult is knowing the damage is□being done and the "professionals" allow it to continue. I've often felt like I'm watching my ex and his family stab my precious daughter, and I am forced □to watch with my hands tied behind my back. So painful.....

Ritamarie:

I feel like I am watching my children on death row, and they are about to be ☐executed forever and I can stop it. Or shooting heroin in their veins and ☐telling them they will be ok, it just a temporary thing.... AHHHHHHHHHHHH

Its like having a loaded gun pointed at your face....☐☐I think the longer you wait to react the worse your chances are for ☐survival.... ☐Again we all are in different stages, but yet walking the same devastating path...

Nancy:

I've had many dreams where my ex is physically hurting (punching/kicking) one of my children and watching helplessly while it happened. I remember feeling incredulous that the kids somehow accepted it. They were dreams and a bit fuzzy but I always remember waking up with this horrible feeling in my heart and stomach.

Joani:

To be honest, there is no reason for us to have patience with PAS when it is a form of abuse. It is no different than having patience when someone is being physically abused. Are we supposed to have patience then too?

My Husband's Story

by Joan T. Kloth-Zanard

My husband's story started when he married his second wife, S, who stole his children from him and his family. Since 1996, he has only seen his children six (6) times and since 2006, he has had no relationship with them at all.

He was and still is a good man and father with strong values and morals for raising children. Yet, his second ex-wife would have none of this. As far as she was concerned, if he was not going to be with her and love her, he was not going to have a relationship with his children either. In her warped mind, she believed she was protecting them from their father and to this day still believes this.

It all started when he met S in high school and she refused

to let go. Even after my husband married his first wife, S would still not let go. When my husband and his first wife's marriage ended, S returned to our home state and tracked down my husband. She lied to him, entrapped him by getting pregnant, knowing that my husband would do the right thing and marry her.

During their marriage, she would put Chris down in front of his children, friends and family. One Christmas, she actually made their two small children (ages about 4 and 6) return every single gift they got from my husband's parents and brother. On another occasion, without my husband permission, she went out and bought a Cadillac with a car loan of $600 a month. My husband had no say in this except to pay the bills. As their relationship progressed, things went from bad to worse.

In fact, S started her rein of psychological abuse with my husband's son, E, from his first marriage. When E would come for his visitation, S would treat him horribly, making him crawl on the floor with his half-siblings, cleaning up after them and taking care of them. E never told his mother or us until he was 16, and then he opened up about how S would tell him his mother was no good and that she was a liar and how he should just come live with them because his mother could not properly care for him. She even went as far to try to get child protective services to take custody from E's biological mother. When that did not work, her abuse of E became even worse to the point that he would no longer visit his father.

Though out this time, my husband was allowing his second ex, S to manage and pay all the bills. He was literally just handing his paycheck over to her, to pay the bills. And she was deliberately not paying all the bills and in particular, his child support to his son from his first marriage. My husband had no idea because she was throwing all of the letters from Child Support Enforcement into the garbage. It was not until they he was threatened with arrest and slapped with a bill for over $16,000 owed in child that he figured out what was going on.

Two children later and the marriage was worse than ever. They separated for three (3) years, during which my husband tried to make the marriage work for the sake of the kids. But the final straw was when S demanded he get his hair cut her way. When he refused, she threw him out of the house. Her need for control was overwhelming. Finally, it was decided they would get divorced using the same attorney to save costs. S thought this would get him to come back to her if she agreed to the divorce.

This is when my husband went on with his life and met me. As soon as S found out, her plans to get my husband back were over and she knew it. They were still in the middle of working with the joint attorney, when without notice, she switched attorneys and filed for divorce without properly serving him. She deliberately gave the sheriff an incorrect address to serve my husband, thus he was never served. But the courts did not know this. They assumed that a proper attempt at service had been done and thus S was able to get a divorce without my husband's presence along with convincing the judge that she should have sole custody since he was not there. On to child support enforcement, where S then lied about my husband income, even without any proof, she was child support at four (4) times the amount he made. The judge did not care that my husband was not there to represent himself or that there was no proof of income. We tried to fight this but to no avail, as we could NOT afford the expensive attorney that his ex's family had paid for her.

What the judge did half right was to give my husband generous and liberal visitation. Yes, an ambiguous, without borders court order for visitation that S could violate at any time. And so it went for the next ten (10) years, with my husband going to court to get his child support reduced, his visitation complied with, while fighting false allegations of abuse.

At first, his ex started by refusing to allow visitation by

claiming the kids were not available. In addition, she would block phone calls and refuse to allow the kids to call. She claimed that it was too expensive to call to two towns away. So we established a toll free number to our house phone for the kids to call on, and still she would not let them. Then she claimed that the kids could not visit overnight on Fridays because they had special TV shows they watched together. The judge told her "too bad, then tape them and watch them another time". Then she claimed that they could not sleep over on Saturdays because they had to go to church even though she had never gone to church with them before. The judge again told her again, "Too bad, then take them to church during the week". But this did not stop her; she just continued to make sure the kids were not available. Either no one was home when hubby would call to pick them up or the kids were not allowed to answer the phone and she refused answer the phone either to make the visitation pickup arrangements.

Finally, my husband filed contempt charges for visitation violations along with a request for a family court evaluation. Panicked that the courts would find out the truth, she filed false allegations of abuse, which she coupled with a false allegation of fear for her life. This last incident occurred when my husband went to pick up his kids, who were again not home. On his way back from their house, he found his ex hiding in her car waiting for him to pass by so she could go back home. He cornered her in the parking lot and told her that she was nasty and what she was doing was not good for the kids. Later he called leaving her am message that he knew what she had done and that he was going to get her, and by that he meant, get her in court. She called the police and claimed that he threatened her life. The police listened to the voice message and told her that it as not a threat on her life, but she did not care and told them she still wanted a restraining order against him. This all occurred just as my husband, my own biological daughter and I had been burned out of our home by fire. The day the sheriff came to serve my husband, we were homeless and just trying to get our life back after the fire, and his ex knew it. We could not add this to our plate of problems and so my husband never went to court to fight the charges.

It took eight (8) months for Family Court Services to do their visitation evaluation, during which time it was proved that there was never any abuse. It was determined that not only had his ex made up most of the story but that anything the kids knew had been told to them by their mother. In addition, not one but two family court evaluators determined that his ex was refusing to accept that my husband had moved on with his life in a positive way and that it was over with her. From here it took another four (4) years, including being threatened with jail and having a pro-bono attorney appointed to get the child support reduced. His ex was even caught committing perjury, fraud and forgery by the courts, and they did nothing to penalize her.

This last incident of the perjury, fraud, defamation and slander occurred during the child support modification trials. During the first trial, it was determined that my husband's child support should be reduced and the attorney generals office, which was supposed to be assisting the ex agreed. The ex was furious; filing a motion to appeal the decision claiming my husband was committing fraud. By the time this second round of child support determination came around, the ex was on her third attorney. During this trial she tried to present a day camp bill for $3600 for the YMCA. I knew this was not correct as my daughter had gone to the YMCA in our town and just like us, she would qualify for financial assistance. Between my husband's attorney and I we found out that the actual cost for the kids days camp was $600. She had taken the bill and put a three (3) in front the six (6). The judge was furious when he saw the actual bill and told her if any one has committed fraud here it was her. But the judge did nothing to penalize her for lying in court, slandering or defaming my husband. And his attorney refused to take the case in civil court to press charges against her so that once and for all she would stop her antics.

This, of course, was not what she told the kids. They were told that their father refused to pay for their bills and now they had no money. And like all the financial issues that over the years my husband would prove and win, the kids would be told a different story and my husband never had an opportunity to correct it until it was too late, since she would not allow him to see his kids.

During this time, my husband never gave up fighting for his rights to have a relationship with his kids. He filed six (6) contempt of visitation violations and non-compliance with counseling orders. Each time the judge did nothing to penalize his ex for impeding on his visitation or the orders for counseling. It was like a slap on the wrist for her contempt of the courts with the judge just issuing a new court order for visitation and counseling for the ex to violate. After ten (10) years of impediments by his ex it was too late. The kids were 16 and 18. They were completely brainwashed and programmed to believe that their father was a horrible, terrible man who never loved them and never would.

In 2006, a final court order was made to get his children into counseling and his visitation complied with. The GAL (Guardian Ad Litem) had court ordered the kids to be picked up after school by my husband. There was just one glitch. His ex had not only included in the children's files, the overturned and expired restraining order, but had hand written in each of the children's emergency contact file that the children's father nor I were ever allowed to pick the children up from school. The GAL was furious when she heard about this and had to write a specific order/letter informing the school that the father was allowed and going to be picking his kids up from school.

But this was not the end of it. As with the other five (5) court orders for visitation and counseling that the ex impeded with, this one would be no different, if not worse for the kids. As with all the other orders for counseling, when she could not get out of taking the kids in one way or another, she would change her medical insurance provider to one that the counselor did not take. She knew we could not afford to pay out of pocket for the counseling as we were also on state medical insurance. So this last time, my husband and I agreed to go further into debt and pay out of pocket for the counseling. But it made no difference at this point. During every session both the counselor and my husband would break down the lies with evidence, making small little steps in their relationship. But after every visitation and counseling session, the kids returned home to their mother who ripped any progress made apart. She told them it was all lies and not to believe it. She would further denigrate their father so that at the next visitation and counseling session, they would be 10 steps further backwards and the kids that much more psychologically and emotionally destroyed with confusion.

After months of no progress, my husband spoke with the counselor and it was agreed that until the kids were out from under their mother, they would never be free to think for themselves. My husband made one last appointment with the children and the counselor. During this last appointment, my husband reiterated to them that he loved them, has always loved them and would always love them. He told them he would always be there for them but would no longer force them to visit or go to the counselors.

This was basically the last time he ever saw his kids. His daughter called him once 2 weeks later asking him to take her summer clothing shopping. Two weeks later it was father's day, not one card, call or even email to their dad. Though he tried to reach out to them on several occasions, as soon as their mother would find out, the coldness and refusal to be involved with their father would start all over again.

If only!!! If only!!!! If only, the courts had put down their foot and penalized my husband's ex, S, when she was caught lying in court. If only, the court had included strict penalties that they enforced when his ex violated the court orders for visitation and counseling. If only the court had ordered his ex into specialized counseling with a specialist in grief and anger that understood Parental Alienation with strict penalties if she did not comply or make progress. If only.....maybe today my husband would have a healthy relationship with his kids today.

~~~~~~~

Chapter 9

Always in My Heart

For my children on Mother's Day 2010

by Julia Greer Moreno

□I think of you in the morning light □I think of you in the darkness of night □I miss you in the morning □I miss you at night □I miss not being able to hold you tight □I wish we could be with each other □NO matter what, I will always love you like no other □

I think of you in springtime when flowers are blooming □I think of you in winter, when storm clouds are looming □I think of you in fall, when the leaves touch the ground □I think of you in summer, when everyone's splashing around □I think of you at Easter when Christ rose again □I think of you on Valentine's day □

Let the truth of truths set you free □Maybe then you can clearly see □You were never abandoned □Or left behind □Those who have deceived you □Have placed lies in your mind □I'll never give up □I'll never walk away □

When you are ready to come home □With me, you'll always have a place to stay □There are many more kids just like you □Who have people who supposedly love them lying to them too □For this reason, my fight shall cease to stop □"For justice for all" shall I shout from the roof top □

For you, for me, for sisters and brothers □For Dads, and Mom's, Father's and Mother's □We may be separated by miles apart □But the bond between us is □Always in my heart □□I love you Sweet Pea and Bubba □

Current Biography

for Julia Greer Moreno

Due to what Julia experienced as a child in dealing with being alienated from her father for ten years and is now reliving the nightmare of her childhood, she started the Joshua Rose Foundation on her son's birthday in October 2006. The Foundation honors her two children, Joshua and Julianna Rose who are now being kept from her by the same woman who kept her from her father during her childhood: her biological mother. Joshua Rose Foundation is a privately funded support network to help teach children and families how to make better choices when it comes to changes in their family dynamics. Their motto is to teach families how to be "Separate but not broken, embracing the Spirit of Ohana (family) so that NOBODY gets LEFT BEHIND OR FORGOTTEN". Julia has used her own experiences and the horror stories she has heard from others to write two courses currently offered by the Joshua Rose Foundation. The courses are offered free of charge with the only request that individuals who participate in their PMP (Parent Mentoring Program) pay it forward and tell others who may need support from Joshua Rose Foundation about the courses and programs offered by JRF so that more children and families can be empowered, educated and informed on how to make better and healthier choices for all those involved in family court matters. She is seen here in family portraits that were taken in December 2011, her first Christmas with her children in 10 years since her journey began. Julianna and Joshua are in the back row, Julianna behind her stepfather, Roy and Joshua behind his mom, Julia.

My Story

by Julia Greer Moreno

My name is Julia Greer Moreno and this is my story....

I am a survivor of childhood abuse, parental alienation, 4 years of childhood molestation, domestic violence and 2 rapes.

Growing up, my earthly mother, Rosann used manipulation, deceit and treachery to keep me from my father for ten years. I knew in my heart that she was not telling the truth. I suffered for it growing up as I paid the price for rebelling against her "truths" and believing what I knew to be true in my heart. My biological mother would seek out her revenge later on in my life but the physical abuse I suffered at her hand would continue up until she kicked me out at age 14, however the mental and emotional abuse continued and still continues to this day. I was blamed for my molestation and made to believe that I was getting what I deserved. I was also just another Cinderella for her to use and abuse.

I am the biological mother of two wonderful children, Julianna and Joshua. God has also blessed me with the opportunity to contribute in part to the upbringing of 3 additional angels- Lisa, Christina and Melissa. I am also a young grandma as our oldest; Lisa gave birth to my first grandchild: Cyrus in June of last year.

I am compassionate for helping others heal and recognize that I heal in the process from my "wounds" from life's battles. I am a parental rights advocate, family rights activist but most of all, I am the daughter of the most high God who has called upon me to help families with changes to their family dynamics that they may learn to be "Separate but not broken, embracing the Spirit of Ohana which is family, which means Nobody Gets Left Behind or Forgotten".

I have always known about Christ growing up. My Grandma Allen was someone who faithfully attended church. My biological mother church hopped so I really didn't get a foundation as a child. I had friends growing up who talked about how they had a great talk with Jesus and I recall often thinking of them as freaks. I did not really come to know God until the situation with my children took place. One person I can definitely say that inspires me and I look up to is my Aunt Peggy. She is my dad's sister. She is a very big influence in my life and she prays with me regularly regarding the bitterness towards my mother. I love her dearly and am so thankful that I was able to reconnect with her.

As a non-custodial mother, it has taken a long journey to get to where I am at in my life now. I was a broken vessel much in need of healing that only God could provide through the sacrifice of his son on the cross. I have come to realize that my children, as much as I love and miss them dearly, were something I had to "give up/or sacrifice to end up at the savior's feet. My life was full of sin and bad choices prior to the situation with my children. I was selfish and often only thought of myself and my wants, needs and desires, this even included my wants for my relationship with a priority, not thinking of others, to include my own form of alienating my children from their father.

It was shortly after my children's father and I divorced, that my mother sought out her revenge. She used the situation with our divorce to come to us both suggesting she would help us both maintain our parental relationships. I knew in my gut she couldn't be trusted but wanting to be the better person, I let her back in my life only to have her take the knife she placed in my back during childhood (keeping me from my dad) to stab me in the heart (using the system to Legally Kidnap my children).

I would not have the relationship I have now with Jesus Christ as my Lord and savior had I not been on the journey I have been on. It is a painful journey, but I know in the end, God has called me to help other families. There are a lot of groups out there within the Family Rights Movement (as it is called) but none of them are helping families based on Godly and biblical principles. It is for this reason that I started the Joshua Rose Foundation, named in honor of my two children, Joshua and Julianna "Rose". The acronym stands for Jesus Organized Spiritual Helpers Understanding All Rejoicing On Spiritual Excellence.

It is my hearts biggest desire to help eradicate one of the cruelest forms of Spiritual Child Abuse called Parental Alienation. The 5th Commandment clearly states that children are to honor BOTH mother and father, not choose between them. It is my goal to teach parents who are separating that they do not have to put their children through an unnecessary cycle of emotional hell by simply learning to work together for the love of their child(ren).

Thank you all for being a part of my story.

Restored Family Connections

by Julia Greer Moreno

Before I post what my Aunt wrote, I want to provide a little history. My biological mother kept me from my dad for ten years due to Hostile Aggressive Parenting Techniques. This also meant I was kept from my extended family members to include my Aunt Peg. Although I did reconnect with my dad at age 19, I don't feel my Aunt Peg and I truly reconnected with my Aunt Peg on the level we have now until I had to go to my grandfather's funeral 8 months pregnant and completely devastated.

You see, my grandfather (my Dad's Dad) died on my biological mother's birthday. I was pregnant with my son Joshua at the time. I was not sad because I was going to miss him, my grandfather. I was crushed because I never really got the chance to have a relationship with him. I am sooo very blessed that my children's dad took the risks he did and my daughter Julianna did get to at least meet him and my Grandma Greer before either of them passed as Scott took several of his 4 day weekends and drove us to FL to see my family. THANK YOU SCOTT for taking those risks and for insisting upon taking me to Grandpa Greer's funeral. This is possible because you cared enough about me to help re-establish those family bonds all those years ago.

There were tons of family and close family friends there who had not seen me since I was very young. I was emotionally charged due to the pregnancy hormones but also dealing with anger, hurt, frustration, as well as JOY of being reunited with so many people who had no choice but to love me over the years.

Now, for those who have gotten to know me, know that the name on my birth certificate is actually JULIE, however, due the verbal, mental and emotional abuse I went through as a child, led me to change my name to JULIA as soon as I was able as I wanted no affiliation to that part of my life.

The only person to this day who still calls me Julie is my AUNT PEG. I LOVE HER to pieces and love hearing her say it.

Ok, now that all that history is out of the way, I have NO HESITATIONS about sharing this as I know my Aunt Peg and rest of my dad's side of the family fully support my everyday work that has now become JOSHUA ROSE FOUNDATION. They know I am an open book with all we've been through and I share openly with anyone and everyone, so hopefully our story will help others to not have to go through what we've all been through, especially my dad who is still sadly alienated from my brother. Here is the note that was included in with my quilt.

"Well Miss Julie Lynn,

Here is your long overdue quilt. I sure hope you like it. When you wash it, make sure it is cold water on Gentle Cycle and a gentle detergent, so then the colors will stay brighter longer.

As I told you, each time you wrap up in this quilt, just think of it as my arms wrapped around you, like when you were a little girl. I am very proud to be your aunt and I am very happy that you are my brother's daughter. I love you very much, and don't you ever forget that.

Now that all the serious stuff has been said, I really enjoyed making your quilt in the colors that you like. I hope I covered them all ok, with a few extras thrown in as well. HEE HEE.

Well honey, you all take care and may God Bless You always.

Hugs and kisses,

LOVE YOU BUNCHES,

Aunt Peg"

If this does not give you hope about family restoration, I do not know what will. I was kept from my dad for TEN YEARS. I now have an extremely close bond with my AUNT PEG that no amount of lies could ever destroy. YOUR Children can come back to you. YOU HAVE TO KEEP HOPE. THERE ARE POSITIVE SOLUTIONS.

If you would like suggestions on how to maintain your relationship or would like help in the reunification process,

please do not hesitate to reach out to JOSHUA ROSE Foundation which can be found by registering on our website at:
HTTP://JOSHUAROSEFOUNDATION.WEBS.COM

For my Sweet Pea Princess on Mother's Day
by Julia Greer Moreno

Sweet Pea
You are my Sweet Pea Princess
And my daughter you shall always be
You have given me many riches
Your mom I will always be

Although we have been kept apart
And others keep us from being together
My love for you is eternal in the depths of my heart
I shall love you now and forever

Some have lied to you
And others deceived me
No matter what you do
Let the truth set you free

It's been 6 long years
Of lies, deceit and tricks
I hope you listen with open ears
And not listen to those who are sick

With loving arms
And nothing but proof
You'll no longer be harmed
For you'll finally see the truth

Anything but truth
You should despise
It's not really love
If it's based on lies

My love for you comes from above
I was given a mission by God
To be your mother
I am very proud
Of you and your brother
I did not give you up
I did not walk away
When you are finally fed up
Your place at home is here to stay

Written by
Your MOM

Valentine's Day for Sweet Pea, Bubba, and My Angel Baby

by Julia Greer Moreno

Valentine's Day has come and gone, but my love for you still carries on

My love for you is eternal, not to be extinguished by things that are material

I could have sent you a gift or card, but right now please now that times are hard

It hurts for us to be so far apart, even though you are always with me, in the depths of my heart.

I try so hard to not let days like these drag me down, but hope and pray, "someday" will soon come around

Today was a day of loss in so many ways, there are not enough words to say to explain my grief and pain and sorrow, in many ways, there is no "tomorrow"

Never knowing the reasons why, or knowing how or when, just know my love is always here and shall be until the end

Second chances ripped away without a glance, never even giving me a chance

To say hello, much less goodbye, I'm so numb and raw, I cannot even cry

Everything I've ever said or done always has come from a point of love

I know in my heart, that God's work is at hand, but sometimes it's hard to wait for HIS plan

I trust the Lord in all that he knows, and sometimes, I know my faithfulness shows

It's times like these when I miss you all the most, that I have a hard time showing the faithfulness thru growth

Just know that no matter what else may come, to the evil

ones plans, we must not succumb

I will be here forever, regardless of others, now and forever, I shall always be your mother

To my babies, most precious and dear, may you remember always: the keys to my heart are the love we share between us even while we are apart

My love is eternal, it shall never fade away, and it will last forever on this and every Valentine's Day

~~~~~~~

Chapter 10

"I Hate My Dad:" A Fictional Monologue

by Kat Lai

CHRIS is 12 years old – either male or female.

CHRIS:

I hate my dad. I know, it's kind of weird to hear that, but I totally do. Dad doesn't get it, you know? I mean, he goes and abandons Mom and me when I'm little, and never looks back. But then, I'm expected to see him, what, like once a month for a weekend? Make nice and pretend that we have this great relationship? Please, it's way too lame! Why should I have to go over to Dad's when he doesn't love me? Oh sure, he goes on and on about how he does, but I know what that's all about. He's just trying to bribe me. He thinks I can't see that, but I totally can.

So, I go and visit with him for two nights and two days, once a month just to keep him happy. And it's okay while I'm there, I guess…

(softer) We have a lot of fun, and he always seems so happy to see me. He'll take me to shows and things that I like, and joke with me about stuff. He'll keep the fridge stocked with my favourite food, and rent movies I like…

(angrier) But then he gets so picky about trivial stuff like what I'm wearing, what I eat or what I watch on TV. Mom says that's his way of trying to control me, and she should know. So, really, I'd rather just be home, y'know? I'd rather be with Mom.

My mom is awesome. We're really close. She tells me everything, like I'm her … what's that word? … Confidante. She told me all about the divorce, and why it happened, how much Dad pays in child custody and stuff, and all the agreements they made about me. She shows me all the paperwork, cuz she thinks it's important for me to be informed. I know how devastated she was when he left. She's told me so many times that if it weren't for me, she'd never have made it.

Okay, yeah, I used to have trouble believing her about Dad trying to turn me against her, cuz I mean, he's my Dad, right? Who does that? But the more I hear from her, the more I see it. I look for the signs she talks about, and they're all there. He hardly ever mentions her at all the entire weekend when we're together. Then there were those few times when I didn't want to go to Dad's. And if I don't want to go, I shouldn't have to, right? Mom was always really good about it and told Dad I wasn't going, but then you know what Dad did? He goes to court and gets them to force me to go. And Mom tells me that if I don't, she'll go to prison! That is so totally unfair and manipulative!

(softer) Sometimes, though? I don't know… I mean he always hugs me when I need it most, even when I'm being really mean to him. He says it often enough about how much he loves me too, and he can't always be faking it, right?

(forces her thoughts back with a small shake) But I know now that it was all just a trick. I mean, if he really did love me as much as he said, he wouldn't have left in the first place, right? And he would pay more child support. I've seen the amount he gives us, and it's way less than it should be. He totally lied about his salary to get away with that, and Mom and I both know it.

(softly again) But what about all the times when I fell, and he was always right there to hold me and tell me that everything was going to be okay? And all the times he comes to my school concerts, or the one time I got a role in the school play? He always shows up when I've got a soccer game too, whether I want him there or not. I usually don't, but he's there anyway. And the way he calls me, "his special little girl/boy"…

(Very harshly) No! He just thinks that if he's nice enough to me and good enough, I'll love him. I know that's what he wants. For me to love him, so that I'll leave Mom just like he did. But I won't. Mom loves me and needs me. I'd rather be with her than with a liar, a manipulator and a cheat. I love her, and I won't leave her, and I won't ever let Dad take me away from her.   Even if it means that I have to hate him.

And I do. I really, really hate him!

(pause)

(really softly) And maybe… if I say it often enough, it'll be true.

~~~~~~~

Chapter 11

I Never Asked for It
by Kathy Turetzky

I never asked for it
And yet it happened to me
I felt I lost my child
And yet he was alive
My child thought I was a bad parent
And yet I exceeded the expectations of a mother role
I felt I lived my life for my children
And yet I was beaten down as a bad parent
I was alienated from my child
And yet I truly loved and wanted my child
I was determined to never give up
And yet it didn't seem to help
I continued anyways
And yet after several attempts
I felt I was in a losing situation
And yet it did happen
I did get my child back
And yet I continue to pray
About all those parents who are still trying
And yet another day goes by
Without your child in your life
And yet you are alienated from your child

Continue to make another attempt

And yet one day it will happen

When it may be the last attempt you have to make

Current Biography
for Kathy Turetzky

My name is Kathleen Turetzky. I am 47 years old and a mother of two boys, age 12 and 15. With the help of intervention of a Guardian Ad Litem and a therapist versed in PAS, I was able to re-establish a loving relationship with my oldest son after the alienation. I also have a better relationship with my ex-husband. Rebuilding the bond with my son took much patience and time. Please don't ever give up trying.

Missing Out
by Kathy Turetzky

Every child deserves both parents in their life

And I feel you are missing out

Every parent deserves their child in their life

And I am missing out

Neither parent should badmouth the other parent

And this causes one parent to miss out

When a child shuts out a parent

And I feel the child misses out

When a parent loves their child so much and wants a relationship

And I feel that child will miss out

We each can make changes so we don't miss out.

We all deserve to be loved and we all have every right to be loved by our parents

Don't miss out.

My PAS Experience

by Kathy Turetzky

I am the youngest of 3 siblings, one twin sister and two brothers. As a young child, I always thought I was living a normal childhood like everyone else since that is all I knew. I lived with my mother and siblings and my father would come home once or twice a year for a few weeks when he was in between jobs. He traveled from state-to-state building smoke stacks.

I grew up understanding that my parents had a difficult life. My mother was born in the Ukraine in 1936. In 1945, when my mother was nine years old, her family left the Ukraine and ended up in "Displaced Persons" (DP) camps in Bavaria in southern Germany. At the end of World War II, there was no recognized Ukrainian state. The United States opened its borders with the Displaced Persons Act. In 1949, my mother's family made their way to the U.S. along with 80 to 85 thousand others. As for my father, his mother died of a heart attack at the age of 36 when my father was 12 years old. My grandfather couldn't take care of him so he was placed in a boy's home until the age of 17 when his new stepmother got him out.

My mother's life became quite complex from working as a nurse at a medical clinic to owning a medical clinic when I was 12. During this time, my father had a heart attack at the age of 46, which kept him at home for six months. I didn't like having my father at home. He disciplined me differently than my mother and I was not used to that. I would have to make my parent's bed which I felt wasn't my job since my mother didn't have me do that. I couldn't do the things I normally did such as swimming in my friend's pool across the street. It was almost as if he didn't know how to discipline me since he simply wasn't around and didn't know how. One time I was fed up and called my mother at work telling her I couldn't go swimming. It was summer, and I was stuck in the house. Her reaction, which surprised me greatly, is to ignore my Dad and go swimming. I was thrilled to death. I got to go swimming. I remember chatting with my friend and her sister and talking badly about my Dad when we were swimming. My mother supported this behavior and allowed me to ignore my father. Today, I know this was the worst approach my mother could have taken. Perhaps she didn't want to deal with it and was busy at work or she had her own issues with my father. There are many better alternatives my mother could have taken such as talking to my father as to what she normally allowed me to do and having him talk to me.

After my father had his heart attack, he changed jobs working as a smoke stack builder and became the owner of a health food store in Hawaii with his brother while we lived in Michigan. My parents were married at the time, but to this day I do not clearly understand if my mother intended on eventually moving to Hawaii with him. She never indicated to me that she would. When I was 16, she flew to Hawaii one day and told my father she wanted a divorce and then flew back to Michigan that same day. My Dad was thrilled she was coming to Hawaii and then to find this out was crushing for him. I know my mother was having many difficulties at the time. She owned a medical clinic with a partner who a partner who was violent and physically abused her.

I vividly recall when my mother wanted my twin sister and I to attend a court session for the divorce. My Dad flew to Michigan from Hawaii to attend but I had no idea where he was staying. I didn't want to go but my mother wanted us there. I was sitting on a bench with my mother and twin sister in the hallway outside of the courtroom and my father was on another bench down the hall from us, facing us, where we could see him. I just sat there without any exchange of words with my father. No hello. No nothing. I felt this wasn't normal. I peeked over to look at my Dad a few times and there he was, all alone. I felt in my heart how sad I was for him that we couldn't talk to him and how alone he must have felt. I knew my mother wouldn't like it if we spoke to him so we didn't. This was very wrong of my mother to put us in this position and then to not tell us to go say hello to our father. I never knew where my father was staying and never spoke to him the whole time he was in town. My father was a peacemaker so perhaps he tried to contact us but was shot down by my mother. I will never know for certain.

Another day my mother came home from a court session and told my sister and I that my father wanted us to live with him. My heart filled with joy at this moment thinking my Dad wanted us. It felt very good to be wanted by my father. Then my heart came crashing down when my mother told my sister and I that he really didn't want us. She said it was that he didn't want to pay my mother any money. I wondered if this was the truth. Since my father wasn't there to tell us otherwise, I accepted it as the truth. This made me very sad since I truly felt my father didn't want us.

The day came when my father was to pick up his belongings from the house. My older brother stacked his belongings in front of the house since he didn't want him to come into the house. I was thrilled my Dad was coming to see us and very disappointed his stuff was being thrown out in front of the house. My Dad came and I peeked out the window to see him. I wanted to go outside and hug him so much. I watched him as he took his belongings and put them in his trunk. I felt so empty inside and thought he must feel twice as empty. I knew if I did go outside my brother would disapprove so there I sat watching my Dad until he took off without having the chance to say a word.

My mother let us know what the court order entailed and how she had to pay my father a large sum of money each year for 5 years for the split of the medical clinic where my mother had 50% ownership. I was bothered and upset my father would take money from my mother when he didn't even work at the clinic. I was siding with my mother for I felt she was the only one taking care of my siblings and me and how dare my father do this to us. Now I have an understanding that usually there is a 50% split of assets when a marriage is dissolved. My father deserved his rightly ownership. No one told me that back then.

My mother was murdered by her business partner when I was 19 years old. My father flew from Hawaii to Michigan and stayed at my mother's home for a few months. He even took the house off the real estate market since it was to be sold per the divorce agreement. During my mother's funeral service, I stood by my mother's boyfriend. This was familiar territory for me. I was trying to make a statement to my father to the effect of, "see what you missed out on?" However, during that episode, I was bothered that I was standing next to my mother's boyfriend instead of my Dad. My Dad was a few rows back from me so I wondered what he thought. Was he even bothered I wasn't standing next to him? I wanted to stand next to him but in my mind, I wanted to let him know how mad I was he wasn't in my life. I wanted a father in my life and he wasn't there. All these thoughts were going through my mind at the same time I was grieving tremendously for my mother. It felt like I was headed for tremendous difficulty in my life ahead of me.

My Dad eventually flew back to Hawaii. Even though we knew my mother's business partner killed her, the police department was conducting their investigation. I received a call one day from a lieutenant at the police department. I know now he was calling to see my reaction to my mother's death since usually a family member is the first suspect. He asked me how I was doing with my mother's death and I told him I wished it were my father instead of my mother. This is the utter contempt a child has when a parent alienates the targeted parent from a child. I am thoroughly beside myself to this day that I would make a statement such as that. At the time, I felt my mother was there for me and lived her life for us where my father didn't.

I completed college without ever asking my Dad for help. He never offered and I never asked. I felt he never helped me during my life ever so why ask, although he in fact did help by sending money home to my mother when he was working out of state. I finished college and afterwards had difficulty finding an entry-level job in Michigan. I was living alone and was yearning to be part of a family again. I hated life. I often said I wanted to die young. I drank often, too often, and was on the way to becoming an alcoholic. I didn't feel life was worth living. One day I decided to move to Hawaii. I sold everything I owned and flew to Hawaii to live with my father. My twin sister was already living in Hawaii with her boyfriend, not too far from my Dad. I spent an entire summer living with my Dad and his wife in Hawaii. I was able to come and go as I pleased without any discipline. Even though I was an adult, I wanted to feel like he cared and this is what I was used to with my mother. The discipline style was very different between my parents.

I would come home drunk many times in the middle of the night to my father's house and nothing was ever discussed about it. There were times I never came home and showed up in the morning hung over and nothing stated again. I would stay at my sister's or a friend's house but I never called to tell him where I was or what I was up to. My life was going nowhere, and I knew that. I received a call about a job offer back in Michigan so I decided to leave Hawaii and do something with my life. I just told my Dad I was leaving. I didn't think he even cared. My sister told me one day shortly thereafter that I hurt my Dad by leaving. That statement bothered me so much since I never knew that. I wish I had known. Now, I truly feel my Dad didn't want to discipline me and risk losing his relationship with me again, as happened when I was a teenager, when I didn't want to listen to him.

I may have spoken to my Dad 15 times in my lifetime after that. I realized I should go see my Dad before something happens to him so my twin sister and I had plans to visit him one particular year. Our plans weren't firm but knew we should go visit him. One day on my way home from work I called my Dad and we had a very good conversation. I told him I loved him and he said the same back. It felt good to hear that. One week later he died. I never got to see him but was thankful I called him and told him I loved him before he died.

My mother carved my feelings I had for my Dad for a lifetime. I did not have the closeness to my father like I did with my mother. My mother wasn't very expressive or loving mother but she raised me. I needed my father in my life. I didn't get to experience that. My father could have helped by telling us how he felt and by reaching out to us. I know now his difficult life and not being shown love as a child made him introverted and lead to his lack of ability to express love. I learned later in life that my mother's family was very negative toward him and this is why he stayed away. He couldn't handle the tight hold my maternal grandparents had on my mother. My mother's family degraded my Dad to me and told me what an awful Dad he was to not be around us. I am now experiencing my child being alienated from me by his father. Now I feel my Dad's pain first hand. I thought my mother's murder was the worst experience I ever had but the alienation of a child from you is just as awful. I am writing my experience so other's can hear it, learn from it and not have to go through what I did. A parent should say nothing but kind and sincere statements to a child about the other parent no matter how much you hate that person. Let a child carve his own view of the other parent. You will create a life of pain for your child if you step in the way of that. A child has the right to love both his parents. My father's love for me was taken away and now it is too late for me to express to him how I felt growing up and how I wished he were in my life when I was a child. This is what I would say to him if he were alive. But it is too late.

~~~~~~~

Chapter 12

Who Will Cry for the Little Boy?

by Antwone Fisher, submitted by Marnie Bushman

I love the movie Antwone Fisher. I had an assignment in school based on the movie. It reminded me of the poem Antwone wrote:

Who will cry for the little boy?□
Lost and all alone.□
Who will cry for the little boy?□
Abandoned without his own?

Who will cry for the little boy?□
He cried himself to sleep.□
Who will cry for the little boy?□
He never had for keeps.

Who will cry for the little boy?□
He walked the burning sand.□
Who will cry for the little boy?
The boy inside the man.

Who will cry for the little boy?□
Who knows well hurt and pain.□
Who will cry for the little boy?□
He died again and again.

Who will cry for the little boy?
A good boy he tried to be.
Who will cry for the little boy?
Who cries inside of me.

~~~~~~~

Chapter 13

No More Daddy
by Nancy Sears

No more Daddy
No more hooks□
No more fear of dirty looks□
Daddy broke his rules of loyalty□
Now my chance for family□□
Dad held them hostage from the start□
My children's precious tender hearts□□
This Mom is thankful for his foils
But does not wish his life in spoils□□
To hold a grudge will never serve□
To honour the children with pure love deserved□□
Ten years of pain on faces show□
But now we're free to love and grow□□
Thank you God and those who knew□
For Faith, Love and Hope to start anew

We Are the Champions
by Queen, submitted by Nancy Sears

□

I've paid my dues
Time after time
I've done my sentence
But committed no crime

And bad mistakes

I've made a few

I've had my share of sand kicked in my face

But I've come through

We are the champions - my friends

And we'll keep on fighting - till the end

We are the champions

We are the champions

No time for losers

'Cause we are the champions - of the world

I've taken my bows

And my curtain calls

You brought me fame and fortune and everything that goes
with it

I thank you all

But it's been no bed of roses

No pleasure cruise

I consider it a challenge before the whole human race

And I ain't gonna lose

We are the champions - my friends

And we'll keep on fighting - till the end

We are the champions

We are the champions

No time for losers

'Cause we are the champions - of the world

~~~~~~~

Chapter 14

When You Thought I Wasn't Looking
by Ritamarie Daley

A message every adult should read because children are watching you and doing as you do, not as you say:

When you thought I wasn't looking I saw you hang my ☐first painting on the refrigerator, and I immediately ☐wanted to paint another one.

When you thought I wasn't looking I saw you feed a ☐stray cat, and I learned that it was good to be kind ☐to animals. ☐

When you thought I wasn't looking I saw you make my☐favorite cake for me, and I learned that the little ☐things can be the special things in life. ☐

When you thought I wasn't looking I heard you say a ☐prayer, and I knew that there is a God I could always ☐talk to, and I learned to trust in Him. ☐ ☐

When you thought I wasn't looking I saw you make a meal and take it to a friend who was sick, and I ☐learned that we all have to help take care of each other. ☐ ☐

When you thought I wasn't looking I saw you take care of our house and everyone in it, and I learned we have ☐to take care of what we are given. ☐

When you thought I wasn't looking I saw how you handled your responsibilities, even when you didn't feel good, and I learned that I would have to be responsible when I grow up.

When you thought I wasn't looking I saw tears come ☐from your eyes, and I learned that sometimes things hurt, but it's all right to cry. ☐ ☐

When you thought I wasn't looking I saw that you cared,

and I wanted to be everything that I could be. ☐ ☐

When you thought I wasn't looking I learned most of life's lessons that I need to know to be a good and productive person when I grow up. ☐ ☐

When you thought I wasn't looking I looked at you and wanted to say 'Thanks for all the things I saw when ☐you thought I wasn't looking.' ☐ ☐

I AM SENDING THIS TO ALL OF THE PEOPLE I KNOW☐WHO DO SO MUCH FOR OTHERS, BUT THINK THAT NO ONE EVER SEES. LITTLE EYES SEE A LOT. ☐Each of us (parent, grandparent, aunt, uncle, teacher, friend) influences the life of a child. ☐How will you touch the life of someone today? Just by sending this to someone else, you will probably make them at least think about their influence on others. Live simply. Love generously. Care deeply. ☐Speak kindly. Leave the rest to God. ☐

~~~~~~~

Chapter 15

Why Do You Do The Things You Do (A Song)
by Shelley Carlisle for her husband

Why do you do the things you do
Tryin' to take my boys away from me
Limiting my custody
Lawyers gettin' all my money
No vacations with my honey

Why do you do the things you do
Tell everyone I'm insane
That you are not the one to blame
It's all my fault, I'm a deadbeat Dad
Responsible for the father you never had

Why do you do the things you do
Hurt me so bad and the boys too
Can't see the error of your ways
Lost in a vengeful haze

Why do you do the things you do
Karma will come back to you
Find you're living your biggest fear
Alone at last all these years

Why do you do the things you do

Creatin' conflict day in day out

Thrivin' on so much doubt

Getting' high all from the stress

Win or lose, you love this game the best

Why do you do the things you do

Never takin' responsibility

Always lyin' that you will agree

Say you don't want drama but then you threaten

Seems Court is your eternal Heaven

Current Biography

for Shelley Carlisle

I am the "2nd wife" of a man who has been steadfast as a father and in court to stand up for the best interests of his kids against his ex-wife who has attempted to alienate his boys from his life. As a mild to moderate case of Parental Alienation, it is still emotionally devastating and extremely financially challenging to keep moving through the lies, manipulation and continual court dates, attorneys, PCs, and therapists, but the boys have benefitted tremendously with more time with us. We are almost at 50% time-share with the help of savvy PAS Court Judges, Mediators, and attorneys. Being strong, persistent, patient and knowing we are doing the right thing for the kids is what is so important, while continually holding an emotional and loving safe space for the children when they are with us.

Chapter 16

Mom
by Sue Ribero

I keep sending these to my children in hopes that the words will touch them somehow.

I know you're hurt and that I'm not your favorite person

I know you're angry and it's all geared towards me

I know you're bitter at this entire situation

I know that if we try there's a possibility

That we can make it through this difficult time

That we can become friends again like before

That we can laugh and play and goof around

That we can enjoy life if we don't close that door

If you just give us a chance to reconnect

If you open your heart like I know you can do

If you release the anger you have inside

If you look, you'll see I'm always here for you

I love you, Mom

PART TWO
SECOND EDITION - 2013

This section begins the 2nd edition of this book of stories and poems from victims of Parental Alienation or as the courts would prefer the term, Custodial Interference. These are the stories of men, women and children whose precious relationships with each other have been altered and severed at some point in time. Some of regained their relationships but with the loss of childhood memories that they can never get back. Others are still emotionally, mentally and physically distanced from the people they love or once loved. We hope that the growing of this book, though not necessarily a positive thing, will spread the word and the stories that interfering and causing unnecessary drama between the children and their other parent or family members is not okay and all too common because of the lack of appropriate handling of these cases.

~~~~~~~

Chapter 17

No One is Immune From Alienation, Not Even The Rich, and Famous Or Brilliant.

"The Intimate Life of A. Einstein"
Taken from excerpts of an article by Walter Isaacson His letters, including some made public this week, show how his personal and scientific struggles intertwined in 1915, culminating in his great triumph that fall. The tale begins with two letters written in early April by Hans Albert (known as Adu), begging his father to visit him and his brother (known as Tete) in Zurich for spring vacation: Dear Papa, Imagine, Tete can already multiply and divide, and I am doing gometetry (geometry), as Tete says. Mama assigns me problems; we have a little booklet; I could do the same with you then as well. But why haven't you written us anything lately? I just think: "At Easter you're going to be here and we'll have a Papa again." Yours, Adu!

Dear Papa, Today we told each other our dreams. Tete suddenly said: "I dreamed that Papa was here!" Then I thought: "It really would be much nicer if you were with us." I can tinkle away on the piano much better now already; not long ago I played a Haydn and a Mozart sonata and some sonatinas. In short, I could also play with you. The examination is approaching now; but at the same time, so is Easter. Last Easter we were alone; do we have to spend this Easter alone as well? If you were to write us that you are coming, that would be the finest Easter bunny for us. We can live here quite well, you know, but if Mama gets ill one day, I don't know what to do. Then we would have no one but the maid. Also for this reason it would be better if you were with us. Yours, Adu The war made it impossible for Einstein to visit them, but he responded to the postcards by promising Hans Albert that he would come in July for a hiking vacation in the Swiss Alps. "In the summer I will take a trip with just you alone," he wrote. "This will happen every year, and Tete may also come along when he is old enough for it." He expressed delight that his son had taken a liking to geometry. It had been his "favorite pastime" when he was about the same age, he said, "but I had no one to demonstrate anything to me, so I had to learn it from books."

Einstein wanted to be with his son to teach him math, but that would not always be possible, he lamented. Perhaps they could do it by mail? "If you write me each time what you already know, I'll give you a nice little problem to solve." He sent a toy for each of his sons, along with an admonition to brush their teeth well. "I do the same and am very happy now to have kept enough healthy teeth."

But the tension in the family worsened. Einstein and Mileva exchanged letters arguing about both money and vacation timing, and at the end of June a curt postcard came from Hans Albert in response to his father's request that he be available on a particular date to go on their proposed summer vacation: Dear Papa, You should contact Mama about such things, because I'm not the only one to decide here. But if you're so unfriendly to her, I don't want to go with you either. We have plans for a nice stay that I'd only give up very reluctantly. We are going at the beginning of July and are staying the whole vacation. Yours, A. Einstein The coldness of the letter was evident by the signature. Hans Albert was no longer signing off with the affectionate nickname Adu, but with the same initial and last name that his father used on formal letters.

Einstein was convinced that Mileva was dictating the postcards, both the plaintive ones that had made him feel guilty and now the one asking him not to come for the summer hike. So he decided to go on vacation with his new love, Elsa. He explained his decision in a July 1915 letter, also recently made publicly available, to his friend Heinrich Zangger, a medical professor in Zurich who was trying to mediate between the Einsteins: My dear friend Zangger, My fine boy has been alienated from me for a few years already by my wife, who has a vengeful disposition, but also is so sly that outsiders and particularly men are always deceived by her. If you only knew what I had to live through with her, you would hold it against me that I did not find the energy for so long to separate myself from her. The postcard I received from little [Hans] Albert had been inspired, if not downright dictated, by her ... When I write to him, I get no response. Under these circumstances it appeared as if I couldn't see the children at all if I came now to Zurich in July, as I was firmly resolved to do.

His first lecture was delivered on Nov. 4, 1915, and it explained his new approach, though he admitted he did not yet have the precise mathematical formulation of it. That very afternoon, as soon as he finished his lecture, he wrote an anguished--and poignant--letter to Hans Albert:

I will try to be with you for a month every year so that you will have a father who is close to you and can love you. You can learn a lot of good things from me that no one else can offer you. The things I have gained from so much strenuous work should be of value not only to strangers but especially to my own boys. In the last few days I completed one of the finest papers of my life. When you are older, I will tell you about it ... I am often so engrossed in my work that I forget to eat lunch.

Nevertheless, Einstein's triumph was tempered by his continued struggles with Hans Albert. The boy told a family friend that he wanted to spend the entire Christmas vacation hiking with his father, but he wrote a chilly letter to his father indicating the opposite: Dear Papa, I will come over New Year's, i.e., from the 31st to 2nd. I don't want to stay longer because Christmas is nicest at home. Besides, I got skis and would like to learn how to use them with my colleagues. The ski equipment costs about 70 francs, and Mama bought them for me on condition that you also contribute. I consider them a Christmas present. Yours, Adu So Einstein informed his son that he was canceling the trip. "The unkind tone of your letter dismays me very much," he wrote just days after finishing his last lecture on general relativity. "I see that my visit would bring you little joy, therefore I think it's wrong to sit in a train for two hours and 20 minutes."

There was also the question of paying for the skis. Einstein was not pleased. He replied that he would send Hans Albert a gift in cash, "but I do think that a luxury gift costing 70 francs does not match our modest circumstances," he wrote, underlining the phrase.

Thus it was that 1915, the capstone year for his theory of relativity, ended with mixed emotions for Einstein. As he put it in a letter to Zangger: Dear friend Zangger, Just now I received the enclosed letter from my Albert, which upset me very much. After this, it's better if I don't take the long trip at all rather than experience new bitter disappointments. The boy's soul is being systematically poisoned to make sure that he doesn't trust me. Under these conditions, by attempting any approaches I harm the boy indirectly. Come, dear old friend, Lady Resignation, and sing me your familiar old song so that I can continue to spin quietly in my corner! ...

Einstein spent Christmas Day in his Berlin apartment. That morning, he took out of his satchel some of the drawings that Hans Albert had sent him and wrote the boy a postcard saying how much they pleased him. He would come for Easter, he promised. To Einstein's delight, his son enjoyed playing piano. "Maybe you can practice something to accompany a violin, and then we can play at Easter when we are together."

The situation within his family also got better--in fits and starts. That following Easter, as promised, Einstein went to Zurich to visit his boys. They were delighted to see him, and he wrote a note of thanks to Mileva for making things go smoothly:

My compliments on the good condition of our boys. They are in such excellent physical and mental shape that I could not have wished for more. And I know that this is for the most part due to the proper upbringing you provide them. I am likewise thankful that you have not alienated me from the children. They came to meet me spontaneously and sweetly.

Einstein then took Hans Albert off alone, as the boy wished, for a hiking excursion at a mountain resort overlooking Lake Lucerne. In a postcard to his cousin and future wife Elsa, Einstein described his joy:

My dear Elsa, Yesterday I went on a hike with the boy and am enjoying very much being with him. He is kindhearted, trusting, and surprisingly eager to learn, and intelligent. My relationship with him is becoming very warm. Kisses from your, Albert

Einstein's relationship with his family would continue to be intense and volatile, with periods of strain and of affection. In order to dissolve his marriage to Mileva, he offered her a deal: if she agreed to give him a divorce, he would give her the money from the Nobel Prize he fully expected to win someday. She considered the offer for a week, then took the bet. And when he won a few years later, she was able to buy three apartment buildings in Zurich with the money.

Young Eduard (Tete) eventually succumbed to mental illness and was confined to an asylum near Zurich for the rest of his life. Things turned out better for Hans Albert. He went to the Zurich Polytechnic, where his parents had met, studied engineering, and later became a professor at the University of California, Berkeley. He would be at the bedside when his father died, 40 years after the tumultuous year when he conquered his theory of gravity while wrestling with the even more mysterious forces that swirled around his family.

Taken from Time Magazine's article by Walter Isaacson, Sunday, July 09. 2006, http://www.time.com/time/magazine/article/0,9171,1211594-1,00.html

Chapter 18

A Story of Extreme Parental Alienation Syndrome
By Amy Sterling
1997 to 2009

This happened to Alan Rodgers, who was married to his ex-wife for 15 years. The couple had three children, who were ages 1 ½, 5 and 7 at the time of the marital breakup. After the couple had been divorced almost two years, I met Alan. We started a relationship and hoped for a blended family based in our love for each other and common interests. He was a successful horror writer and editor who was establishing his own book publishing company. I was (and am) a science fiction, fantasy and non-fiction writer and college teacher. My other career has been as a non-profit executive and development officer. I had one daughter who was 5 years old at the time I met Alan. During our 10 year relationship, we had a baby together, Anthony. Alan and I never married due to the extreme parental alienation and criminal activities of his ex-wife and her husband.

#

My daughter (age 20) and I survived incredible trauma related to my former boyfriend Alan Rodgers' extreme Parental Alienation situation. The blame that can be placed on me is that I failed to comprehend the seriousness of the situation until it was too late. I truly did not know or realize how bad this type of thing could get until it was too late. I foolishly thought my stability, good friends and hard work/ethics could "combat" this disaster. No. I was wrong and my daughter and I and my baby paid a horrible price.

In Alan's case, his ex-wife married a man (stepfather) who was the instigator. Alan's ex-wife is now a convicted felon. In 2009, she pled down to felony child concealment from felony child kidnapping and received 3 years' probation and a suspended sentence, as a result of kidnapping Alan's youngest son for 18 months, as well as his middle daughter, who was "dumped" with the stepfather's mother and enrolled in school as a "homeless" child to conceal her identity.

In the midst of the 10+ years of extreme abuse, legal shenanigans and alienation activities that impacted all of Alan's friends, relatives and myself, Alan and I had a turbulent relationship and did not live together continuously. Some of the harassment behaviors included work-related harassment and clumsy but frightening attempts to "frame" Alan for various crimes. For example, an anonymous package of child porn photographs was mailed to Alan's place of employment, addressed to "A.R.," his initials. The package was taken to "Accounts Receivable," where employees opened it and immediately called the police who contacted the FBI. Alan (and others by those initials) at the company were questioned by the FBI. I was called at home and questioned by them as well and I followed their directions to search Alan's computer for child pornography. I found nothing, and the FBI agents found no evidence of anyone asking for this package at Alan's work. When I mentioned the custody battle to the agent, he said, "Oh! That's probably it." So Alan did not "get in trouble," but it was extremely alarming and frightening. This was one of dozens of incidents. Any time Alan requested to see his children, a similar incident would occur. One of the most disturbing things about the child pornography pictures was that the FBI agent stated they were known as part of an operation called "Candyman." This large investigation eventually ended up in the arrest and conviction of 40 pedophiles, including 20 Catholic priests, in several different states. So, the person who sent the material (very likely the stepfather of Alan's children and the primary alienator – the package was mailed from a nearby county where he had a temporary job, and speeding tickets, at the time) had to have gotten the child porn from an organized internet child porn ring that led to many arrests.

Another example of these activities included over 100 false calls that were made to the Los Angeles County DCFS. The great majority consisted of one page reports of a phone call that had no factual information, and they were never investigated because the custody battle was well-known to the authorities. During the first part of our relationship, the stepfather sued both Alan and myself, falsely accusing us of the exact activities he was pursuing frequently (trying to get us fired, making false statements to employers, calling authorities with false accusations).

In 2003, I was leaving Alan for the third time, to give my daughter and myself a fresh start away from the trauma. But before I could close the deal on the house I was buying for us, I became unexpectedly pregnant. At the time we had not been sexually involved for several months, and it was a "one time thing." I also have the news for people that if they think it's "ok" to have unprotected sex "just one time" - it's not.

I decided to stay with Alan and have the baby so he would have the opportunity to be a father to the baby - yes, because he had suffered so much trauma trying to be a good father to his children in the face of years of alienation abuse. If I had left, my baby would still be alive. He would be a happy young boy today.

Our baby Anthony was born with Down Syndrome in July, 2004. I also knew ahead of time it was likely Anthony would have the syndrome. We talked with and counseled with Alan's 3 older preteen/teen children about this. Alan's ex-wife and her husband were as negative as possible and tried to instill fear of and hatred for the baby because he was "different." In one example of the stepfather's frequent internet harassment, he wrote a message to hundreds of people who "followed" his mailing list that babies with Down Syndrome should be aborted. These statements were mild compared to the hatred Alan's children heard about the

75

baby in person. To these children's credit, they were loving, caring and kind to Anthony during his short life.

On January 11, 2005, I was on my second day of work at a fulltime job I had taken to provide health insurance for Anthony. On my way home from work in extreme LA traffic and pouring rain, Alan mistakenly thought I'd be home "immediately" when I was two exits away on the freeway and left Anthony by himself on the bed. Anthony became entangled in the covers and suffocated.

Alan's ex-wife and her husband were thrilled. At last, they thought they had the perfect thing for their campaign against him. They told authorities that I had murdered the baby, my daughter (age 12 at the time) had murdered him - and of course, Alan had murdered him too.

PAS is horrific for the "2nd wife" or girlfriend, and any other innocent children involved in blended families. Alan's children were abusive toward my daughter because they were raised in such an abusive environment. Finally this horrible tragedy occurred and of course, none of Alan's 3 children know what really happened. They only know what their mother and stepfather have lied to them about.

When the courts ordered these two to stop their alienation activities and return to normal visitation, they kidnapped the children. It went on and on - well, the children are now young adults, and Alan's ex-wife was finally convicted of her bad activities - but too late for any type of reunification. The family moved 12 times in the 10 years I knew Alan and the later moves were combined kidnapping and forced moves to evading bill collectors and other financial responsibilities. These 3 alienated children have also been alienated from their own mother's family, and have only had contact with their stepfather's mother and sister (as far as I know - as of 2009-2010). Just as my daughter and I suffered years of terror, Alan's children must have suffered a thousand times worse. It is absolutely tragic.

Alan finally suffered a series of strokes, in large part due to the stress. He has not seen his children since the final court adjudication in 2009 at which time only his youngest son was under age 18. He is in a long-term care hospital and will never be able to live on his own again.

The years of stress and fear and exploitation of my baby's death and daughter's trauma finally pushed me over the edge. I was diagnosed with PTSD and received treatment. My daughter too suffered trauma and is only now recovering fully. She found Anthony unconscious and was there throughout that terrible night. Our humanity and any type of dignity were nothing in face of this nightmare.

This was one of the worst child custody cases short of murder in LA County for years. And the person who lost his life was the most innocent, precious life imaginable. Anthony's nickname was "Lali" and we call him "A pure spirit of love." And he was and is. I worked in the nonprofit field during this time (assisting homeless families with children) and had worked in that field prior for 10 years. Never, in all of my professional work with thousands of troubled families, had I ever seen or heard of something of the level of this, the length of time it went on, or the extreme deviancy and dysfunction of these "parents."

There is also a health impact on Alan's alienated son, who turned 18 this past December. I and Alan's sister attempted to contact Alan's ex-wife, to tell her to take Abram for genetic testing. Alan's father (the boy's biological grandfather) had a genetic condition that caused severe mood swings, and circulatory and heart problems. Alan clearly has the disorder as well. He is 53 and has suffered three severely debilitating strokes. If he did not receive 24 hour medical care, he would certainly suffer a fatal stroke. Signs of this illness had begun to develop in Alan before I knew him - so in his 30s.

Of course, the mother does not respond or seem to care. Alan paid for top quality health insurance (Kaiser) for all 3 children for the entire time I knew him, and continued after the court adjudication and beyond age 18. He had saved money for all 3 children's college. All were declined by the mother and stepfather - who preferred to keep their children in a transient, deprived lifestyle. The children had free, high quality medical care that was never used in any way. Now that Alan is in the hospital, he still thinks he is paying for their health insurance and still anticipates paying for their college, even though he is permanently disabled and probably never "coming home."

Alan and I never had a chance as a couple, nor was there ever any chance to "blend" families. We were dealing with two hardened criminal mentalities from day one. Alan dealt with it since the day in 1997 that the stepfather drove a U-Haul to Oregon and together with his wife-to-be, kidnapped her three very young children for six weeks.

Alan was at work at a low-paying job to support the family and came home to find the house totally trashed and his computer stolen - with a note that said "I've left. Don't do anything stupid." That level of judgment and behavior continues to this day.

From the very beginning, all of Alan's children exhibited numerous behaviors associated with emotional abuse, physical abuse, neglect, and even sexual abuse. Although all were and are very bright children, they all missed a lot of school, with two children falling behind at least one grade. The oldest daughter suffered the least academically and was able to receive mentoring and support at school. She was able to attend and graduate from UC Berkeley, clearly with scholarship aid. Despite false information ("I work 90 hours a week and earn $100 an hour") provided continuously to authorities throughout the process, the stepfather has not worked at a steady job since 2002. Alan's ex-wife, formerly a respected book editor, burned every personal and professional bridge she had during this horrific circumstance. She worked briefly as a Los Angeles School district teacher, but never completed her credential and did not pay off her extensive student loans. With a felony conviction for child concealment, that career path is closed to her.

In addition, professionals should know that the extreme behaviors of the stepfather and mother frightened many people who were involved with the case over the years. Only the final Family Court judge, Frederick Shaller, was not intimidated or frightened, and understood the scope and depth of what had occurred. He spoke about the unspeakable and permanent, lifelong damage done to the children. He said that he hoped someday the children could read the court proceedings as adults and know that their father loved them very much, and they would learn the truth.

The couple was aided in their legal harassment and manipulation of the cumbersome and complex court system by an attorney from the Los Angeles area who was not well-known in any courthouse, or by any other attorneys. He did not seem to have much of a legal practice, and just filed motions and false harassment lawsuits that appeared to be written by the stepfather – a man who portrays himself as a "genius" and "computer expert," who is in fact, an unemployed high school dropout whose computer skills are more than a decade out of date.

Alan's final attorney believed that Mr. Smith, the attorney who facilitated the abuse, "shared a vice" with the stepfather. Considering one of the "framing" attempts was sending child pornography to Alan's work, yes, we did all decide this was a likely candidate for what the "vice" was. Mr. Smith turned the couple over to collections for their initial bill in the amount of $20,000, yet returned years later to try to cover up for the felony kidnapping. He only stopped when he was informed by Judge Schaller that he would be charged as an accessory, and that a complaint would be filed with the Bar Association. At that point, Mr. Smith left the courtroom and was not seen or heard from again.

Alan was awarded full custody of his children during the time they were kidnapped. Only his youngest son was actually kidnapped. His oldest daughter was a young adult already in college. His middle daughter had been dumped with the stepfather's mother and was attending school under an assumed name. To this day, there is no way to know where Alan's youngest son really was during the year and a half he was kidnapped. The parents and the boy stated they were in both Canada and Mexico for extended periods. However, the boy came back speaking no Spanish of any type. He had missed school for over and year and his mother, who lies about her educational attainments and qualifications, stated she was "home schooling" him.

All of the incidents and crimes committed would easily fill a "true crime" book. All I know is if the fear that I and my daughter felt during this time was any indication, Alan's children must have suffered unbelievable terror. They never had a secure home physically, emotionally or spiritually. They were torn from all real family members, never had the opportunity to make friends at a school for any length of time, or live in a normal home. Most of all, they were raised in an atmosphere of complete, criminal dishonesty and a constant conspiracy to harm others. Not just their father, me, or my daughter or their baby brother. Everyone these people came into contact with was a potential victim.

None of the "schemes" were ever successful in the long term. Except the alienation. Alan is all alone in a long term care hospital. His children either do not know, or do not care. There's no way to know what they think about what happened to their little brother who died. The only certainty is that they do not know the truth, and probably never will.

#

Readers should know that these behaviors are cyclical. People often ask how I maintained any relationship with Alan, and did not run away after the first incident with the stepfather, and the first fake lawsuit, the first move to evade court adjudication, and the constant, never-ending petty battles that will be familiar to all going through Parental Alienation at any level.

First, I sensed the children were in trouble. I cannot turn my back on any child in need under any circumstances. Second, Alan did his level best and dealt with the situation with his own form of courage and fortitude. He was never late for a pickup or drop-off for visitation. He sacrificed many things for his children. He kept his mouth shut in the face of extreme, frequent provocation on the part of the stepfather, and later, even that man's mother. Yes, he was in denial until the very extreme incidents occurred after Anthony's death. After that, he did understand what he was dealing with, he was in fear for his life, and was in fear for his children's lives. Then, he tried to find his son because he truly felt his life was at risk and was in fear for his safety. This is why he persisted to attempt to get the legal system to work.

Financially, this situation cost me personally well over $100,000, and it cost Alan far more. It contributed to Alan's strokes and disability. It cost my baby his life.

I was myself alienated from my own father by my grandmother for extended periods of time. I was also subjected to a situation of extreme fear at home while growing up. Alan also grew up in a dysfunctional family.

Therefore we were both vulnerable, more so than people raised in stronger, more functional homes. In Alan's case, he lived in perpetual denial about the devastation his children were enduring and the ways in which they were suffering and acting out. In my case, I falsely told myself I could "deal with it" and handle it long after any well-adjusted person would have stopped. I made the decision to stay with Alan when I became pregnant for the right reasons morally. Yet in a practical sense, my baby would still be alive today if I'd gone ahead and moved to that little house I'd bought for myself, Anthony and my daughter.

In terms of time and life, this situation took some of the best years of my life from me. It cost my daughter emotional trauma and incredible tragedy. She found her little brother unconscious right ahead of me. She picked him up and laid him on the bed. She was in a home where three extremely emotionally disturbed children ganged up on her with all the manipulation, verbal abuse and sickness they experienced in their mother and stepfather's home on a daily basis. She saw these children get attention, and when they didn't get as much as they constantly craved and needed – manipulate and act out to get it – and all the normal, healthy behaviors she was raised with seemed to be ineffective. Fortunately, she has recovered and continues to recover and grow stronger and happier every day.

I think of these children as raised as "People of the lie." There is literally nothing that the stepfather and mother haven't lied about, don't lie about, or wouldn't lie about. Not just the alienation, in all areas of life: financial, business dealings, work ethics, and even simple household duties or holiday celebrations. Instead of whatever the stepfather brings home doing casual work, he "Makes $100 an hour and works 90 hours a week." Instead of the modest apartment the family lives in, it's a "6 bedroom house." A weekend trip to Mexico is "Traveling months in Mexico."

The stepfather is "a personal friend of Al Gore," and says he predicted that President Obama would become president way back in the late 1980s. He says he played high school baseball with home run champion Mark McGwire. The truth is, the stepfather is a high school dropout and Mark McGwire played high school baseball for a private Catholic school. It is all lies. Alan's children have been alienated and estranged from their mother's family as well as their father's family. All are isolated alone with the stepfather and his family: a classic pattern of abuse.

Alan's ex-wife too has paid a heavy price for this relationship. She is a convicted felon. Her appearance is haggard and much older than her years. At one point in time, she was a well-respected book editor. If she did not have many friends, she did have colleagues and associates in the industry. She had a large family and has little to no contact with them. After she left Alan for the stepfather, her career began spiraling downward. She has worked only sporadically since 2000. In one of her last court appearances before the final, 18 month kidnapping (there were many shorter-period kidnappings prior to this), she told the judge, "I cannot work. My youngest children are 7 and 9."

No, she could not work because her 24-hour, 7 day a week job was following the orders of a mentally deranged malignant narcissist. She could not even care for the children properly under those circumstances, much less hold down a job or have a normal family relationship or friends. This woman has been in a prison under the control of a maniac since 1997. Unfortunately, she has brought three children (now young adults) with her, in addition to two younger sons she had with the stepfather.

The "system" was inadequate in this case. But I tell this story for another reason. Any women who are involved with men facing PAS, or men involved with women facing PAS, or same-sex couples, should be aware that they cannot allow themselves to be victims, and must not let innocent children that are not part of the custody battle be victimized. I am not a defenseless victim with no insight or capacity. Once I realized that I was facing enemies who did not care whether or not I was married to Alan or what my relationship was, I took charge of my own safety and that of my daughter. This is why and how I know so much about this couple. It only took one false lawsuit that cost me $15,000 in legal fees to convince me to protect myself and Meredith.

The "system" allows people like this to continue for years – yes. However, in addition to manipulating the Family Court and child support systems in two different states and three different counties, the couple also has a list of creditors that is three pages long. They have left a string of disgruntled landlords in their wake, and at least half a dozen destroyed properties. They refinanced their vehicle: twice. The "children's advocate" may have found these people to be suitable parents, but that was without ever visiting any domicile where they stated they were living and based in no facts whatsoever. They are both long-term unemployed and a high threat for "slip and fall" or any other type of lawsuit abuse, but hardly "successful criminals" or scammers.

None of these behaviors ever occurs in a vacuum. No parent would ever undertake the extreme PAS behaviors as occurred in this case and in others if that parent is a stable, reliable and dependable parent. When the situation is this bad, the parent can only be depended upon to harm the child. Authorities who fail to recognize this are allowing one of the oldest, simplest abuser, scammer, and fraudster tricks in the book: accuse someone else to deflect suspicion and attention elsewhere.

PAS may be a suite of behaviors common to dysfunctional parents. It may be something they choose to do because they can, and because it serves a very real and pressing need. They don't just want to hurt the target parent. They want to evade scrutiny and suspicion because they are hurting the children in real, specific, direct ways in the form of abuse and neglect. They want to keep the children from talking not just to the target parent or other family members. They want to keep them from talking to authorities, counselors, teachers, and others as well. They embroil the child in a web of lies, of which PAS and the target parent is just one small part.

I am,

Amy Sterling Casil

13 March 2013

Aliso Viejo, CA

~~~~~~~

84

Chapter 19

To My Little One, Our Heavenly Bond

3/8/09
For: Justin Martone
By Mom Cheryl Martone,
From Westbrook, CT.

You are sacred and you are blessed my dear
Every second you have to know you are love
By your mother who holds you near
The Lord our God is watching. He is love from above.

You can walk with your head held high
I (we) pray for you always and everyday
Learn that evil lurks out there, don't be nigh
Use your intelligence, that you are right in a way.

Of most importance, not in a shadow
You can start to stand on your own to stay
with your family, we will meet in the meadow
To stay with us to hold us near and pray everyday.

We can understand and be a friend
You are in our hearts and there you be
He is our spiritual blessings in the end
Worth it our spirits are together, ties you with me.
Love Love Love My Mom
XO XO XO XO XO XO

I wrote this poem for my son & dedicate it for all the children who are separated & alienated from their caring/loving parents, as my child was by DCF/CPS illegally. It was at a time when they were keeping him from living with me for their own selfish reasons and it was written because my Mom never saw my son, her grandchild, after he was kidnapped in March 2008 by

DCF/CPS, she kept asking for him, she was too ill to go to him, until my mother passed in Jan. 2009.

~~~~~~~

Chapter 20

From Out Of Nowhere...A New Beginning

12/21/12

Eric Larson

Although I've been a member of the group for quite some time, this is my first post and my introduction to the other members.

I was a single father with sole physical custody for 7 years when there was a knock on my door. Looking back it was that moment, the decision to open the door that turned my world upside down. I, like all here found myself trying to comprehend, navigate, and survive the unimaginable. A campaign of alienation, the Family Law system of ??? □(Santa Clara County, California) lawyers, mediators, evaluators, Dr.'s all the alleged "Professionals", what action to take.....etc. For me a 10+ year battle, thousands upon thousands of dollars, supervised visitation, then nothing, you know the story. With the last 5 years having practically no contact at all with my son. During the past 5 years the miniscule contact I did have was by way of email and consisted of hostile remarks, allegations of the bizarre, absurd, and most definitely untrue. In my attempt to understand things I sought information, advise, I researched, joined this group, I searched internally, and learned all I could. Seeking justice, peace, love, my sanity, a way to fill the emptiness and at times it seemed I was fighting for my very existence. We all do the best we can with the tools and information we have at that moment, right? Everyone's case is different I know, the following is a quickly written summary of my experience thus far. Hoping to possibly provide a small ray of light to the alienated who see the light of hope fading and those fully lost in darkness of alienation....... □□

I chose to end the legal battle (right or wrong) after 6+ years, step off to give it some room and some time. This was one of the hardest decisions I've ever had to make and I questioned this decision in the years of no contact that followed. ☐☐

I'm trying to keep this short, void of details and just spit out a sentence or two that somehow says "hold on, there's always a chance" or something similar. I am finding myself reliving events and how it's almost impossible for others to understand how shredded and hollow you may feel. How cheesy and meaningless even the most sincere offers of hope people relay to you can seem............. It's not working, I can't think of anything to say that would ease anyone's pain nor can I offer a plan or proven course of action. I wish I could. I can share this:

On December 22nd 2012 I received a phone call from my SON. He asked me if I could meet him in a few hours, he wanted to talk. Of course I agreed. I was surprised at my feelings regarding the meeting. Five years ago I would have been doing back flips and been excited. I found myself calm and with no expectations.... or maybe I didn't allow myself to feel excited or feel anything at all. I learned long ago that for me to survive in my world of alienation feelings were not something I could afford to show, or even have, period. To point out the obvious, this method of survival is not conducive to long or healthy personal relationships.

My son had a Doctor's appointment close by and we met an hour before his appointment time. I imagine the fact that he had given an hour towards this meeting with a definite out (the appointment) combined with the fact I had become an emotionless imposter in my own life aided in my apparent lack of excitement. Was it that? Or was I afraid of what f#$%ed up garbage might spew out his mouth this time? Maybe. But maybe not. I then realized I couldn't care any less about the past. The past is exactly that, "the past" there is no life there, it's gone. All I saw was the present and an unwritten future. Shit, that meant I had hope. I was unaware hope still resided in me until that moment.

Anyway........................□□

I decided not to move in for a hug when I approached him but instead offer him the same handshake I would offer any man that I respected but with the added light kind of arm grab thing some guys do that to me express more care or love. We both said "good to see you" as the distance closed and then, there we were. After five long years... I □executed the handshake as described above... which he accepted but also continued in a gave me a big hug, I hugged him back of course, stuttered a bit and said he looked good and that I've missed him or something. We got a coffee and talked. I was surprised how comfortable our conversation was, even though we were both choosing our words carefully and maintaining some unspoken but easy to determine boundaries. At least that's how I experienced it. □□

Again, I'm really trying to keep this short. The details are not going to help anyone but myself. What's important is that it happened!!!!!!□□

Moving forward............. □□

We ended up spending the rest of the day together talking, but not of the past. No "why this" or "how could you that". It seemed surreal; we were together talking, hugging, laughing, I guess you could say getting to know each other......better or perhaps, again. It was late and time to go our respective ways, he gave me his phone number and in my mind I was doing back flips, it seemed amazing to me to have my sons phone number. And he wanted me to use it, to call!! WOW, something most folks do every day or think nothing about just seemed incredible. Which is sad but at the same time huge? Saying goodbye was hard for us both I think and as he hugged me again hard he said, "I'm so sorry Dad, I can't explain what" his voice was breaking up. So I cut him off saying "You don't have to say anything, we're here, I love you" something along those lines. He asked what I was doing tomorrow and if we could get together again. Which we did. He told me he was moving out of state, soon. He was waiting on a trucking outfit to provide a driver for the trailer they had packed the house in but he felt it would be after Christmas. Then asked if we could spend Christmas together!!! Holy S#@t yes we can, in two days my world had changed so much. It was hard to believe. He called me Christmas Eve about noon and said the driver called and was going to be there at six that afternoon, he had to cancel our Christmas plans but asked if we could spend the hours before he had to leave together. Which we did. We both relayed our desire to maintain our current course and agreed to keep in phone contact. We came up with "penciled in" plans to visit each other. Right before he got in the truck while hugging me he says "I love you Dad and I'm really happy that your still you after......" I said something to let him off the hook and did good holding in the emotion (as I have experience with this) to make it easier for us both. As he drove off the feelings of loss made a brief appearance only to be quickly and fully destroyed by the happiness and amazement of having had the past two and a half days together. Two days that changed my world. It seemed so easy and all those years lost such a waste. I can never know his experience and may never know how he was lead to doing and saying the things that had caused so much heart ache. That is perfectly fine with me. If I could take the confusion, pain, regret, and guilt that boy has dealt with or may still have to deal with; I would do it in an instant. Even without the 2 1/2 days that brought us together again. All of us in the world of the alienated would. We have enjoyed daily phone contact from the 22nd on.

Final thoughts.......................□□

I don't know if I conveyed the massage I intended or if I even produced a proper sentence in this post. My message is this: When you feel lost in or consumed by the inky blackness that is life in the world of the alienated, think of this story and know there is still a chance. Sometimes doing nothing can be the right thing, as stupid as it sounds. I'm not suggesting you do nothing just not to consider backing off as failure. □□

I'm not a legal professional, a doctor of any kind, not a counselor, social worker, or enemy infiltrator hired by your ex. I'm a father who had lost a child, himself, almost all hope and then for reasons unknown was granted a miracle.

I don't know what our future holds, but I now believe we have one. □□

"A NEW BEGINNING" □

~~~~~~~

Chapter 21

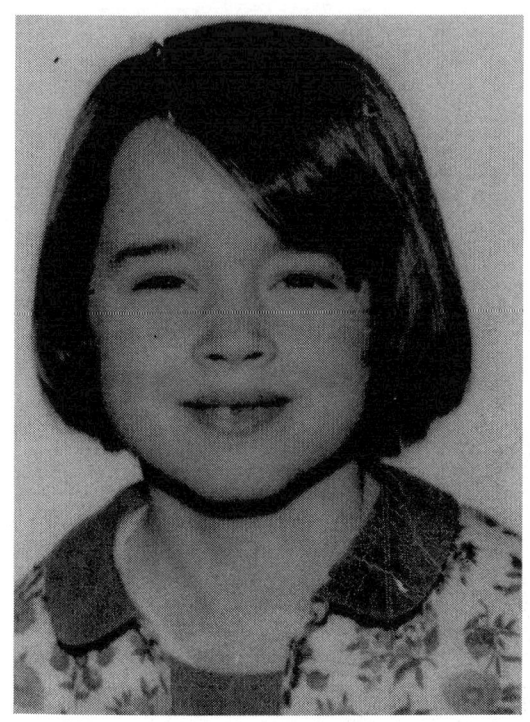

Gina's Story

By
Gina Hines Whelan

My parents dated in high school, and my mom became pregnant. My parents married, and shortly after the marriage my father joined the Navy. My mother's father did not like my father's mother. He alienated my mother because of this. But my mother lived with my father's mother. My dad returned from the Navy, and worked as an insurance agent. My mother stayed at home with the children. My father's mother worked for Howard Johnson as a realtor, and my father's father was a dentist. My dad's parents divorced when I was three years old. I loved seeing my grandfather! Unfortunately his visits were few, and far between. My older siblings say he was an alcoholic.

All of us children were born fairly close together. I am number eight out of ten children. The tension between my mother, father, and his mother was palpable. My parents would fight, and one day when I was three years old I was in the kitchen, and I saw them fist fighting. I screamed at them to STOP, and they did. We left my grandmother's house because the situation became intolerable with fighting, and arguing between my parents. My mother was five months pregnant with her 10th child when we were panned out to neighbors. Fortunately I went to my aunt's house, and I remember having a lot of fun with her. Thanksgiving of 1964 I was reunited with my family for the day. Ironically we had Thanksgiving dinner at a Howard Johnson's restaurant. Christmas eve of 1964 we moved into a three bedroom housing development apartment. My Christmas presents were donated by strangers. But it was a bad area. I was eventually molested by the neighbor across the street in 1965. I was four years old.

I missed my dad a lot, and he would infrequently visit. My dad used to call me "princess" he showered me with love, and attention. Mom was a different story. One day, I was so excited, because my Dad was coming over. But then my mom came up the stairs to my bedroom, and said, "Your father is not coming." She just turned and walked away. I could not understand at such a young age, what I had done that he would make him not want to see me. I was literally crushed.

Mom started going out, and drinking at bars with her girlfriend. My older brother was "in charge," but he could not replace my mom. One evening I was really sick, and my mom went out. For hours I waited for her to come home. I sat on her bed with my head on the windowsill hoping the next set of car lights would be my mom. Finally she came home, and when I met her at the door I fainted. Sometimes my mom would look at me and tell me I was "constipated" when I wasn't! It did not matter; a soapsuds enema would ensue. By the time, I was 6 years old, I knew that I needed a break and just went to overnight camp to get away for one month. I did not miss my mother at all during that month.

My older siblings claim that my dad was an abuser, but I think mom picked up where he left off. You never knew when the "other shoe was going to drop." My mother used a leather belt on my bare bottom. I felt humiliated, and demoralized. There was nothing I did that warranted that abuse. As I became older the abuse was physical and verbal. My mom would be sitting at the table as I was walking away and she said "Hey Gina" as I turned around she was giving me the middle finger. It was not uncommon for mom to take her shoe off, and throw it at me.

The last time I saw my dad he was in the intensive care unit of a hospital. He was on a ventilator that was keeping him alive. My mom made the decision to discontinue the breathing machine. My father died of lung cancer when I was 12 years old. Ironically I was smoking cigarettes when he died.

Eventually I moved to LA and started working to work as a Playboy bunny. But I was determined to be more than just this and so while I worked I went to school to complete prerequisite courses for nursing at the local college. Hugh Hefner even paid for my books to attend these classes. Eventually, I moved back home received my Associate's degree with the help of student loans.

When I turned 40 I was tired of smoking (a pack a day). I got on my knees and prayed because it was time for me to turn my life around. I had spent enough years burying the pain I felt from the loss of my father and grandfather in my life along with the molestation. So I stopped smoking and started running so I would not gain weight. I ran my first marathon, and qualified for Boston! Since this time, I have run nine marathons, four of them Boston and I qualified for each of them.

In 2007 I decided to go back to school graduating Magna cum Laude with my bachelor's in nursing. I am now working on my Masters in nursing education with only two classes away from graduating.

From my pain and hurt, I have grown and learned. The biggest lesson I learned was that I will NOT allow the past to determine my future. My future is mine.

~~~~~~~

Chapter 22

Heather's Story

By Heather Swicked Elaine Kent

From Heather's Youtube video:

http://www.youtube.com/watch?v=F-6ILtb63fl

Hi everyone, my name is Heather. I want to tell you my story of parental alienation.

My parents went through a divorce when I was around 9. At first, I stayed with my mom most of the time. Even though my parents fought, mom and I would always go to my dad's house for supper. This lasted for nearly three years.

In those three years I was very close to my mom. We talked about everything. Eventually, my mom found love again. With Chris, my mom wanted to fulfill a childhood dream of mine; to live on a farm with horses.

But I couldn't stay there.

Just as I started Grade 7, the judge gave primary custody to my dad. When my dad told me this, I thought he made it up. That night, he ranted until 3 AM about how 'the courtroom was cheering when the judge said I was to live with dad.'

He told me my mom was furious and stormed out of the courtroom. At that time, I would only see my mom on weekends and she could call every night. When I saw my mom that weekend, I was scared of my mom being angry at me...

Instead, we both began to cry...

In January 2007, Mom and Chris married. I got two new stepsisters too.

At the beginning of Grade 7, all the kids thought I was weird because I liked horses so much. They called me Horse Girl. Some days I went home in tears, so I began to hide myself...

I started to dress 'emo'. I wore black eyeliner and started draping my hair in my face.

Eventually I did find a group that accepted me for me.

But I still wore my mask. It wasn't just for school bullies anymore...

As the days went by, my dad took to ranting about my mom late at night. These talks would last from 9pm until 3am.

He wanted me to push my mom away.

Every time I was on the phone with my mom, my dad would be standing right there. I couldn't have a private conversation with my mom, so I tried to avoid talking to her for long. I used to watch the clock on the microwave and end the conversations once they lasted longer than two minutes.

Every time my mom dropped me back off at my dads from spending the weekend with her, he would lecture me and demand to hear about what I did over the weekend. When I didn't say much, he would accuse my mom of talking to me about court.

If I would tell him that mom didn't talk to me, he would tell me that I was a liar and he would just get angrier until I gave in and told him what he wanted to hear.

But my mom wasn't the only problem I had with my dad.

My dad raised four boys; a girl with a smaller stomach was not what he was used to. He would insist on filling my plate with more food that he even took for himself. When I barely finished half, he would accuse me of being anorexic and trying to starve myself.

He started to yell at me until I finished my plate. One night, I ate so much that I threw up. But that only made him angrier, which made me miserable. No matter what I did, I was a liar to him...

So when I went to my moms for the weekend, I was sullen. I would spend all of my time alone, because it was the only place I could be without getting yelled at. I would barely eat, because the sight of food made me feel sick. All of this terrified my mom...

I started to push my mom and her family away. I had to do it...

It was the only way I could survive in dads house...

The only place I was happy was when I was with the horses.

Horses don't yell.

It didn't take long before my dad started to make me write emails to my lawyer. I had a lawyer when I was in Grade 6 but I never emailed her until then. My dad said that he wanted to get rid of the phone calls every night. Not wanting him to start to yell and rage if I said no, I agreed.

When they went to court, my dad got just what he wanted; the phone calls were gone. Instead, I would visit with my mom on Thursdays for a few hours.

But to him, that wasn't good enough...

My dad started to tell me things about my mom. He told me that she didn't love me, that she thought I was a hassle to go into the city to spend time with. And I believed him...

I began to despise my mom. I didn't like to be with her when my dad had told me all of these things about her. So when she wanted to get family photos taken...

I didn't smile.

Then my dad introduced me to Marie.

At first, I didn't care about Marie. Then she moved in with my dad...

It all seemed like it was going to be ok. When Marie moved in, dad got mad at her quite often and he didn't lecture me as much. Unfortunately, it wasn't going to be that simple.

Marie, getting sick of being the target for my dads anger, decided to burn off some steam herself. I became her target. She didn't see me as my dads daughter...

I was competition for my dads love.

Soon, she began to insult me. She called my clothes and even my walk 'slutty'. It didn't take long for my self-conscious to get the best of me, so I started wearing baggy clothes. A lot of my clothes were men's clothing...

According to her, I was selfish, rude, and into drugs.

I've never even touched a cigarette. I was scared that it would affect my training as a cross-country runner. But that didn't stop her.

Marie told my dad that I was sleeping with numerous guys, that I smoked, drank, and probably tried drugs. He believed it.

I was 14...

It hurt me when she said those things but I couldn't cry.

It all came back to horses...

I felt stronger with horses...

Somewhere where no one could touch me. And that was very comforting.

I leased a horse at a stable close to my Dads house. Before, my mom went riding with me on Fridays. Now, my dad insisted on taking me to ride on Tuesdays. Tuesdays were my favorite day. Horses were able to calm me. Everything that was going wrong in my life didn't matter there.

The next school year was a blur. I managed to make the city championship for cross-country running and came in 33 out of 300 kids. I also came in first in hurdles. It made my dad proud...

It wasn't enough. My dad refused to let my mom attend any school events of mine. I was also in Band, but whenever I had concerts, I couldn't stay to talk to my mom or look at her. I had to run backstage, put my instrument away, and get into dads car.

If I didn't, my dad would start yelling at my mom...

When the school year was coming to an end, I didn't want to go to the Grade 9 graduation. My mom and dad were already arguing about it, I felt so awkward when both of my parents were in the same room. The tension in the air was overwhelming.

My friends convinced me to go, it was quite important to us at the time and they didn't want me to stay at home alone. My parents both went, my dad on one end of the gym and my mom on the other.

This made my dad furious...

The lectures got more aggressive, more emails were sent between my mom and my lawyer, it just felt like a downward spiral.

With Grade 9 at its end, I had to pick a high school...

I chose a school called W.P. Wagner. Most of my friends were going there but I also chose Wagner just because I felt comfortable at the school. I loved the programs, the teachers, and it was just a great fit for me and the things I love.

In order to try to be close to me, my mom took a job that was close to my school. Some days when my dad was dropping me off at school in the morning, we would pass her on her way to work.

Sometimes, my mom would smile and wave at me. I wouldn't wave back, I didn't know what my dad would say if he caught me, but I knew it wouldn't be good.

Instead, I tried to focus on school to take my mind off of my parents. In Grade Ten, my friends from Jr. High and I started to drift apart. Some didn't go to Wagner and the others started to hang out with other friends. I didn't make, as many friends as they did, but the two most important friends I made were Porscha and Jeff.

We were the Three Musketeers.

Having friends like Porscha and Jeff made me happy, when I was down they were right there to pick me up and keep me going. Unfortunately, I wasn't allowed to hang out with them a lot. My dad didn't allow me to go see my friends very often.

Still paranoid about the things Marie was saying about me, my dad didn't want me to even take the bus to and from school. I wasn't allowed to go to parties unless the parents were supervising, he had the parents' numbers, and he also had the names and numbers of each of the kids that were attending...

Because of this, I didn't even bother asking to go out anymore. All it would do is get me accused of trying to drink or do drugs. It used to frustrate me so much; how can I prove to you that I'm not a bad kid if you keep believing all of the things that aren't true?

I started to get depressed. I felt completely powerless in my life, not trusted for unfair reasons, and on top of it all; I would get lectured about Court and about my mom...

But again, my friends were there to save the day. One Saturday morning, Porscha and Jeff, came by bus to get to my house, at 6am and knocked on my basement window to take me shopping with them.

It was honestly the best surprise I ever had that year... I felt so happy to have such amazing friends...

After that day, I wanted to hold onto my friendships even more. I wanted to see them more. Most of the time, I would just see my friends at school; sometimes I was even allowed to bring them over.

Those days were the best.

My dad thought I was spending too much time with friends yet I rarely spent any time with them outside of school. Like horses, being with friends took my mine off of my family issues and made me feel at ease. I hated to be at my house with my dad because I knew it meant more lectures.

I hated being involved. All I wanted was to feel normal and to feel like a kid, with all of the issues with court, I felt like I was being forced to grow up. In a way, I think that's what my dad wanted. In order to make the judge believe the lies my dad made me write to my lawyer, I had to seem grown up.

I busied myself with extra curricular activities to avoid going home. I stayed in Band when I went to High School, but that still caused problems when both parents wanted to go to my concerts or volunteer to help with Band Trips and etc.

So I joined Leadership.

In Leadership, we had a big fundraiser for the year called a Bike-a-Thon. It was a 24-hour event, so we stayed at the school overnight, I was also the school mascot, so I would get in my costume and run around the school. The mascot costume was the best; I kept getting hugs and high fives. Everyone was excited to see me. I felt like the life of the party!

After that, I met Damian. We began dating around the end of the school year. When I first introduced Damian to my dad, Damian shook his hand and said, "It's nice to meet you, sir", and later on my dad told me he thought Damian was rude, just because he said "Sir".

My dad never approved of him.

Marie would tell my dad not to trust me and continue to accuse me of sleeping with everyone. After that, my dad didn't want him at the house, and he wouldn't let me go to his house or out anywhere. The only place we could be together was in school. Because of that, it made it very hard to have a relationship. We ended up dating off and on throughout High School, which depressed me. All of the high school drama was getting to me...

My dad told me that Marie was practically my mother so I tried to talk to her. Yet everything I said, she told to my dad and he would yell at me about it and tell me what I should and shouldn't do. I knew that I could no longer trust Marie, so I found that I was left with one other person other than my friends; my mom. Occasionally, I would talk to her about school, but I was still very wary to trust her. I still believed what my dad had told me about her.

When I visited with my mom on Thursdays, I always asked if we could go look at books or wander around the mall. After a while, I liked Thursdays; they were a day when I could get a break from my dad. One day, we went to Chapters. I was wandering around when I noticed my mom talking to an author doing a book signing. In the car my mom told me what they were talking about...

The man claimed to be a 'Mystic'. He told my mom to not worry about me, that I would return to her when I'm 16. He also predicted things about my brother and sister, but what he said about me stood out. At the time, I thought my mom was just saying it so I would spend more time with her. I didn't tell dad about the Mystic.

My dad had other things to rant about anyways.

He wanted to get rid of Thursday and weekend visits with my mom. Every time I came home from spending time with my mom, he would say that mom talked to me about court. That I 'looked' like she talked to me.

By that point, I was getting roughly 4 or 5 hours of sleep a night, because of my dad talking to me late on school nights. I was falling asleep in at least one class a day.

I didn't want to be kept up every night so I learned to mask my emotions in front of my dad. Sometimes it helped, other times I got yelled at anyways.

Things got even worse when my grades went from A's and B's to B's and C's...

My dad was furious, which I expected. But his reasons for being mad was that the court was going to blame him for my marks when it's my moms fault...I didn't understand that, my dad had me the majority of the time anyways...

It felt like my dad was more worried about Court than he was about my marks in school...

My dad always insisted on e-mailing my homework for the weekend to my mom. After that, he started adding in extra assignments. I would be stuck doing homework all weekend. Most of the extra assignments were things I couldn't even do yet. The teacher still needed to teach us how to do them.

Eventually my mom figured it out and started to ask the teachers to e-mail the homework to her instead of dad e-mailing her. Then my dad asked them to e-mail him too. To me, it all felt ridiculous and embarrassing knowing my teachers e-mailed my parents...

A few weeks later, I got called down to the school office. I was nervous to see if it was my mom. My dad told me that if my mom came to the school, I had to keep away from her.

My mom had made a meeting with my English teacher to discuss my marks. I didn't want dad to find out so I did what he told me to do if I saw my mom; I ran.

My mom looked horrified that I ran away from her. She started to follow me at a walk, but I kept going.

Eventually I did slow down because people were giving me weird looks. When my mom caught up to me, she hugged me, told me she loved me, and that she would see me later. She looked so sad...

I knew my dad would be proud of what I did, but I felt ashamed. All I could think about was the look on my moms face as I ran away...

When I told him, he told me that I needed to tell my mom that I didn't want to see her again. He told me exactly what to say and how to react...When my mom got me later on; I did as I was told.

Then my mom started to cry and asked "Why?" I couldn't say anything...Dad didn't tell me what to say if she asked 'Why'.

I realized that it wasn't what I wanted at all. My dad was just using me to hurt my mom. And that disturbed me.

I realized how much I missed my mom.

When I got home, I avoided my dad. I didn't feel comfortable around him anymore. My house wasn't a home any more; it felt like it was suffocating me...

I started sneaking out my window late at night. Not to do anything bad, just to walk around and be away from that house..I knew that I had to get out of there fast.

The clock was ticking, and if I didn't do something, my dad would take over my life.

When my parents went to court later on, the judge ruled in my dads favor. Thursday visits with my mom were gone and I would see her every second weekend.

At school, I called my mom up to have lunch with her...

She told me that if its what I wanted, she would respect that because she loved me and she didn't want to fight anymore if I didn't want her to.

All of a sudden, I was very scared to lose my mom.

I planned to move out on October 14th. My mom didn't believe me at first, but the more I talked about it, the more she realized that I was serious.

My two best friends offered to help and my mom found a place for me to stay; an old coworker of hers offered to let me stay with her.

I was grateful for all the help, but when October 14th came, I was scared. I considered calling it all off...Then Marie called me a b*tch...that was the last straw for me. I wasn't going to put up with that anymore.

I started packing, I was extremely nervous. By the time Porscha and Jeff got to my window at 11pm, I was in hysterics...

Porscha came through the window to calm me down and help me pack the rest of my things while Jeff stayed outside the window and put everything into duffel bags. We were done by midnight. I left a note for my dad, saying that I moved out and I would explain tomorrow. Then I crawled out that window for the last time.

We jogged down the road, the dull thud of the duffel bags hitting our backs filled my ears. I was still shaking and scared, but seeing my friends running on either side of me gave me courage. I couldn't have done that without them...

A couple blocks down the road, Jodi, my mom's coworker, was waiting in her car to pick us up. She was amazed that we made it...

Jodi drove us to our new home. By the time we got in, we were all exhausted. I asked Jodi if Porscha and Jeff could sleep over, she said yes. My sleep that night was dreamless. The next day I awoke to chaos...

I had numerous angry messages from my dad and Marie demanding that I come home that instant. I tried to call them but my phone died. When I charged my phone, I called my mom to talk to her. Then, the doorbell rang. It was Jeff's mom, coming to get him. When I let her in, my dad walked around the corner and let himself in.

He started to yell, told me that I was not doing this, and made me go get my things from my room. I was still on the phone with my mom, she heard him yelling and called Jodi and told her he was in the house.

I was crying as I packed my duffel bags. My friends were taken outside. Then I remember Jodi say, "You are trespassing. Get out."

My dad tried to grab my arm but I backed away behind Jodi. This was a new rage I had never seen before...

Jodi escorted my dad out, but unfortunately he had taken all of my bags except for one duffel bag of clothes. Then he started yelling at my friends...

Half an hour later, Porscha came in. My dad wanted her to convince me to go outside...

It turns out, when my dad got my note, he started calling everyone claiming I ran away. When he called Jeff's mom, she took pity on him and since she was going to pick Jeff up, she let my dad follow her to the house.

I did not run away. When I moved out, I was 16. In my province, any child over the age of 16 is allowed to move out. In special cases, children the age of 14 are allowed to move out. I had confirmed all of this with my school counselor. I couldn't believe my dad accused me of running away...

I couldn't let my friend go back out there, so Jodi gave Porscha some money and called a taxi for her. Porscha took the back door and used the walking path behind the house to get to the closest gas station and she went home.

Then, Jeff came inside. My dad also wanted him to convince me to go outside.

Jeff told me that my dad was demanding information from them on how I did it and why. Jeff wouldn't tolerate being bullied and refused to talk. However, Porscha caved and told him what happened. I was upset that Porscha had given in, but I understood how hard it is to stand up to my dad when he's angry.

Jodi said that we needed to go to the Police to report my dad for trespassing and see what we could do. Jeff went back out to his mom's car and Jodi and I went to the closest Police station.

The Police refused to help us.

When the investigators interviewed Jodi and I separately, they told Jodi that she had to apply beforehand if she wanted Guardianship of me. Jodi, thinking I was mature enough to not need a guardian, said she wasn't applying. When the investigators talked to me, instead of bringing up guardianship, they just told me that Jodi wasn't going to let me live with her.

The officer was trying to convince me to move back with my dad. Instead, I asked my mom to pick me up.

When my mom picked me up, she told me that Jodi did want me to live with her. The investigators tried to trick me...

My dad used to be a Police Officer and he was quite popular with other Officers. My mom told me that one of the investigators was a friend of my dad, which would explain why he tried to fool me...

It took nearly five months for me to get the rest of my clothes and belongings back from my dad.

After I moved out, my family on my dad's side refused to talk to me. My brothers were getting married and having children and I would have to find out through Facebook.

For a long time, I wanted to bring Justice to all of the things my dad put my mom and I through. I was disgusted with his actions and how he manipulated everyone around him.

I wanted to fight with everything I got. But I remembered something my mom told me; she said that at one point she had to make a choice. Should she fight for what is right or should she fight for our relationship? That made me think...

My dad loves the fight in court. He loves the conflict and beating people down. He loves to yell. He loves manipulating people and getting his way. He loves pushing people over the edge and driving them into a blinded rage to try to prove that what he says is a lie. And in order for him to be happy, he always needs to be fighting someone...even if its his own daughter.

When you think about it that way, do you really want him to be happy?

I know I don't.

My best revenge for what he did is to simply live my life and enjoy being free...

I am the master of my fate... I am the captain of my soul.

I got my mom back.

I graduated.

I got my High School sweetheart back. Now we're engaged.

I got my family back.

And I'm starting to get my other side of the family back too.

I'm still in love with horses, as always. :)

But the most important thing is that I'm happy.

Thousands of kids experience what I have experienced.

It IS abuse.

This is one story out of many and my hope is that the more I tell it, the more people will listen. The more people will see.

My hope is to help as many people as I can with everything I have learned in this situation.

~~~~~~~

Chapter 23

A Family Tragedy: A Mother Asks When Will The Torture Stop?

By Ina Watters

How It Happened:

I was married for fifteen years to an abusive (verbally and physically) alcoholic. I lived with an Order of Protection. I had three children, two boys and a girl. I just couldn't stay in it any longer so I filed for a Divorce in 1978, the children then being 10, 12 and 14. When he was served with the papers he started working on the children, telling them what to say if they were interviewed in the Judge's Chambers, "say you want to live with your Father". They were not allowed to get in my car, sleep in their beds (he kept them down in the basement with him). They became silent and stopped talking to me. They wouldn't eat if I cooked only if he cooked it and I was not included in that! They were afraid of him so they co-operated and did whatever he wanted them to do. He must have told them quite a story about me and of course being so young they bought it all!! He had the money power so it was easy for him to manipulate and twist their minds. It was a very subtle undermining under-handed manipulation and he went to the extremes!! They were his little Army!! While living in that house during the Divorce it was very difficult. When the Divorce was final and I won the case on the grounds of Cruel and Inhumane treatment and too unsafe for me to co-habit with him we had to live in the same house for nine months after the Decision came down, then the house would be put on the market and sold and divided. This is what took place next:

The Destructive Behavior!!

He was very upset at the results of the Decision. The kids started a destructive pattern. I was locked out, salt was put in my tea, the light would be turned out if I was reading, the stove would be turned off if I was using it, if I was doing laundry that would be thrown out in the front lawn. If I was curling my hair that curling iron would also be thrown out in the front lawn. They would put hand cream all over my car. They would stand in the driveway with the garden hose running so I could not get out of my car! My room would be pulled apart and everything thrown on the bed!! When I went to pick my daughter up from dancing school he would be there too so she would run to him. My ex would take my daughter to work in case I might talk to her when he wasn't there. The last time I visited the house I got a flat tire, the air out and I had to call a tow truck (this was the last time I went there). My ex was bent on breaking me before I got away from him. There were a lot more destructive things happened!! We got joint custody, the boys to live with him and the girl (because she was under 11) got to live with me. He took her out of school one day behind my back and took her to his attorney to have her sign a paper about her custody. Then he served the papers on me when she became 11. After alot of thought I let her go to live with them as she wanted that so badly and I just could not hold on to a prisoner!! My ex violated the visitation (as well as all the other Court Orders). I was shut out and never seen the kids for years. He went to the extremes. When all the occasions came up, Confirmations, Graduations, Birthdays, Christmas, Easter, etc. they would go silent and I would be ignored. It hurt very badly, the PAIN was unbearable, to be out there on my own abandoned and not one caring what was happening to me -- was the worst!! When my daughter was with me he would call her and tell her the plans (I wouldn't know them), he would pick her up on a Friday with the boys in the car - **no** I didn't get to have the boys at all!!

The Three Hostages:

My ex did get re-married to a neighbor who lived near them. I didn't know this but I had a way of finding out!! They were married 8 years then he found an old girlfriend he used to have and then told the wife TO GO!! The kids were held like hostages with him without any contact with me at all. I couldn't even get through to them by phone, so I knew little about them and how they were doing in school, etc. All the functions I would go to at school, church, etc. but I was not included, ignored!! When my daughter was graduating from Nursing School she asked me would I pick her up? I was aware of the pattern and I knew this was a "build up to a let-down" so I said I could not. She was going to do like she used to do when I would pick her up from dancing school - just run and go with her Dad!! So I avoided this PAIN! I was there and shook her hand and congratulated her!! Her Father of course was standing beside her - he had to take the credit for everything!! It appears that they enjoyed doing this, of course the more destructive things they did to me the happier my ex was and they would then be in his "good-books"! My ex is in a Nursing Home now after having three brain operations (tumor removed)!! I just say, "he was the devil and those were the ingrowing Horns!!" The kids will go to see him at the Nursing Home, which is in the same town as I live in - and pass me by!! I can't understand how they are still so loyal and attentive to him at their age? I guess this is a Life-time Sentence and they will leave it until it is too late and my life will be over, I missed out on so much of their lives already?

Adult Children of PAS:

Although the kids are in mid-life they still give me the silent treatment and are very loyal to him. Even though they know what happened and what he did. I can't understand it, they never call and truly I cannot say they've been sons or daughter to me. They still continue what they were doing when they were under his roof!! I cannot understand!! Very neglectful, I cannot accept their behavior any longer, what I get from them is NOTHING!! It is very sad, they were my whole world - it crashed and now I have to turn this negative into a positive, I need positive SUPPORT and feed-back from the PAS group. I'm glad I have found it!! **I informed Child Protective Services about this subtle cruel child abuse and Brainwashing. We had an interview with a Therapist in White Plains. He had worked on the kids and again told them what to say. So of course they said all the right things that Dad told them to say!! That Dad was great and there was nothing he was doing, it was their Mother and my daughter said "she should be thrown in the Garbage"!! The result of this interview was – That I was the Perpetrator and that the Father was ok!!! THIS IS CHILD PROTECTIVE SERVICES!!!–** Maybe they should get a copy of this and/or your BOOK??? Thank you.

A VERY SAD, FRUSTRATED/ABANDONED AND ALIENATED MOTHER!!

Ina

~~~~~~~

Chapter 24

Just The Skeleton of a PAS Story
By Joy Morgan

On Feb. 2, 2002, a SAC CPS worker showed up on my doorstep on a weekend I had the kids. When she told me who she was, I told her I had the children and she was not welcome. She told me if I did not let her in, she would take the kids. I let her in which was not good because they had to hear everything. I was accused of hitting my then 7-year old daughter in the head with a hammer. I asked her when this happened and she said when I built my desk. I told her that was over a month and a half ago. 2 weeks before Christmas break. I told her if I had hit my daughter in the head with a hammer, I would have gone to jail when I dropped off the kids at school that Monday morning and that she would have needed medical attention, which she obviously did not and she would have had a wound on her head which there was none.

When I denied hitting my daughter in the head with a hammer, I asked the CPS worker to bring out my daughter to ask her. Unfortunately, my daughter said in a singsong voice. "Mommy, you did hit me in the head with a hammer." I told her, Mommy does not remember hitting you in the head sweetie. Then the CPS worker turned to me and said I was trying to brainwash my daughter by denying it. I sent my daughter back to the room. I was only telling the truth. Next, the CPS worker told me that I was also allowing the children to be exposed to Frank and Shirley Weckman who had court orders not to see their own grandchildren. I told them that was false information that I have been friends with the Weckmans since I moved to Rio Linda with my then husband who still lives in Rio Linda. I was told that their daughter, Lee, now lives with my ex-husband and that my ex is now alienating Lee and her two children from her family. The CPS worker then told me to stop taking the children to see the Weckmans or I would lose custody of the children. I did, two weeks later.

I know my ex was part of the brainwashing because months before he tried to show CPS and the court a picture where my daughter had a bruise on her arm smaller than the size of my thumb. I knew he was up to dirty tricks back then and he complained to the judge that no one listed to him. However, get a child to tell the school (and they are mandated reporters even if they do not see bruises) and they have to call CPS. So after this incident, I lost custody because a narc/BPD/bi-polar/sociopath had to have control no matter what. He repeated his alienation with his first fiancé, Lee, when he alienated her and her two youngest children from her parents who lived just down the street in Rio Linda. All the documentation I used, the police report on my ex when he beat my oldest daughter (they even took pictures), the doctor's note showing my black eye, declarations of co-workers who saw me come to work with black eyes, or wore turtlenecks and long-sleeves in the middle of summer to cover up bruises on my neck and arms, declaration of the Weckmans of the alienation of their daughter, Lee and their two youngest grandchildren from them, and a declaration of the parent of my daughter's friend when she ran away from her father because she was terrified of him. Well he brainwashed my oldest daughter to deny she was afraid and that she ran away because she was a rebellious teenager who did not want to pay her part of her cell phone usage.

Additionally, when I went to trial in 2010 (and the last time I saw my kids or spoke to them on a regular basis), I told the judge that my ex violated joint legal custody by taking the children to a counselor without my knowledge or written consent (someone CPS picked out naturally). I wrote in my trial brief and request for orders to strike her letters submitted to the court (and I recall that my ex did not subpoena her as a witness). The ex objected. The judge wavered. I stated that she did not know the DV history of the case or the police report of abuse dad inflicted on our oldest daughter. The judge stopped me and told me "Never say that again." (Mind you this was in front of a court reporter.) He said he did not want to go to trial. I had subpoenaed my forensic evaluator with a psych eval that showed I was not crazy but suffering from effect of abuse and that I was not a threat to the children, my supervisor of 6 years who observed me and the children and my ex, his first fiancé that he alienated from her parents down the street, the fiancé's parents (Frank and Shirley Weckman), and the parents and best friends of my oldest daughter because my oldest daughter ran away from her father and wanted to come live with me. They wrote a declaration how terrified my daughter was of her father.

I still have my oldest daughter's e-mail dated 06/23/2008 just before we went to court in 08/08 where I was going to ask to increase my parenting time (I was briefly off supervised visits and we had normal times except they were brainwashed into thinking I was weird and irrational). My oldest daughter asked to live with me full time during her senior year since she was taking AP chemistry and she wanted me to help her. I have my BS in chemistry although I changed careers from a pharmaceutical QA chemist to become a paralegal because of my loss of the children. When we went to mediation, she walked past me and would not look at me. The mediator was different this time and he treated me like a criminal. I asked her what happened and she said she remembered why she did not want to live with me. More brainwashing. I have supervised visit reports where all the children asked to come home with me, my son asked me to hide him so he did not have to go with his father when our visits ended, etc.

However, after my trial, my own supervisor told me to stop going back to court to gain custody and to even stop seeing the kids altogether. She said my ex is an aggressive narc who will do anything to emotionally harm the children. I haven't seen them since March 2010. Any suggestions. I have been so heartbroken. I have left messages every Saturday telling the kids I love them and I am proud of them. Except March 16, 2013. I called, but no answering machine picked up so I now do not have a way to contact the children if I do not know where they live.

This is only the skeleton details of my case. I believe that CPS is behind the court ensuring that my ex always wins. I paid $12,000 in 2002 for a psych evaluation. The evaluation did not have the test results. Those were completely left off. Although it showed my ex had issues, the point of having the test results is to prove that I was telling CPS the truth that my ex had issues and they wrongfully took the kids away from me and that he at the time of testing also alienated his current fiancé and her two youngest kids. So I was not the only one he actively alienated. His personality disorders drive him to complete control.

All the people I subpoenaed in my case told me not to. They were terrified that my ex threatened them that he would file a CPS report on them. I believed that CPS would help him. Additionally, documents that I filed in my case disappeared from the court file. I attached court orders, exhibits with the previously mentioned declaration, police report, and copies of my supervised visit reports that showed the kids asked to come home with me and my son on more than one visit asked me to hide him so he did not have to go home with is father.

At trial, all of this evidence would have been recorded, but the judge very conveniently made sure there was no trial. I spent a lot of money on process servers to serve the subpoenas to get everyone's testimony.

I have suffered heartache after heartache. I don't have any more money to pursue my case.

Additionally or Finally, I want to say:

As the result of the abuse on me, the children have suffered abuse, which is what I have been trying to tell the courts all these years. I have also requested over and over that the children need counseling and so does he. He absolutely refuses to go to counseling and even though there have been orders for the children to attend counseling, he refuses to take them and has brainwashed the children into not wanting to go to counseling because they do not have time because they have homework and after school activities.

Bottom-line, he does not want counseling because he doesn't think anything is wrong with him and he does not want anyone to know the truth about him and the children. He doesn't want the children to go to counseling for the very same reasons. I am the only one who has followed court orders: attended counseling, attend co-parenting classes, attended DV classes, attended parenting classes, and even attended other classes that were not ordered or required by the court. My ex violated every single order ever made. Although my ex and I fought horribly during the marriage (mostly me getting beaten or screamed at), I would scream back in my defense and sometimes in my way to abuse him since I was only 95 lbs to his 220 lbs, I hurt him the only way I could: I told him I hated him and I wished I never net him and I knew why everyone in his family hated him, too, and why Jamie (his ex-girlfriend) kept his daughter away from him and that he did not deserve to have kids if he beats their mother in front of them.

I eventually left because I literally woke up every day wanting to die. The only thing that kept me alive were our children. I did not want them to have to grow up without a mother and I believed WEAVE counselors (Women Escaping a Violent Environment) when they said if you leave your abuser, the abuse eventually stops because the abuser has lost control. Boy were they wrong!!! and need to be educated on narc/bi-polar/borderline/anti-social/sociopathic behaviors. These are just a few of the disorders that my individual counsel believed my ex husband has. She told me that I have to stand up to every lie my ex accused of me but I could not show emotion or weakness. She said that I had always to fight back as soon as he falsely accused me or he will continue to run me over like he did in our marriage. And that is what I have done. She is the one who told me about Bill Eddy and his books. I have one of his books, "Divorcing a Narcissist". Unfortunately, nothing has worked with him. Nothing.

Because of my Christian upbringing, I prayed for him. I purposely never called him ever. I only dropped off and picked up the children before and after work. He was the day care provider and then he worked nights while I worked days. We kept the children out of day care this way. However, he used every excuse to come out and verbally attack me and make threats against of taking the children or even sometimes threats against my life. I called the police each time, but they would not do anything because the threats were just threats. I filed from TRO, but it was denied because they were just threats. Meanwhile, the attacks continued and when I drove off to ignore their father, my oldest daughter would tell me that I was rude that I did not talk to her father or listen to what he said. I told her that I was not going to stay and be yelled at and that one day I hope she will understand. I also told her that I hope she will one day have a boyfriend or a husband who would not yell at her at all and would speak to her with respect and that I wanted someone to speak to me with respect. I never called their father any bad names. I did not yell back while I had the children. Unfortunately, as I previously mentioned, I did have to call the police on more than one occasion. WEAVE told us to this especially if we did not call the police during our marriage. We needed to start and make a record.

I will write the rest of my story. I have a 22-page document, but it is not accessible right now. It is on a computer that was cyber attacked and it is possible that my ex was a part of that as well. I have been stalked; I have had messages left on my answering machine of conversations that occurred in my home and not on the phone. I feel that he somehow bugged my home or was able to record through the computer. I do not know. I do know the children had cell phones and they even told me that their father could hear every conversation we had when the children were with me. It gives me the creeps just thinking about not being safe in my own home ever!!

~~~~~~~

Chapter 25

A Christmas Present to My Children
By Julia J Berghold

I have the Christmas blues. I don't think it's more than last year although I think I'm more aware of it this year. I feel the pain and the lose more than last year. Maybe it was worst last year, I don't know because I felt nothing last year.

I just realized some of that pain came from material things I gave my children in years previous. I was grieving for what my children have lost. The fact that I couldn't buy as much. Couldn't give them as much.

I kept wondering and wondering how to make this up to them. For I have a hard time giving them what they need at times not just what they deserve. So I started thinking about what they need and how to make it special. The answer came as a shock to me they'd give it all up if mom felt better.

So what I decided to give my kids along with a few things they need is a new Mom. I can't go back to the one they remember and love. Nor do I want to. She suffered in silence to long. But I can give them a stronger mom, financially better off mom. With this being said I am going to therapy. I am better than I was but still have a long twisty road ahead. I will learn how to make a website. Get my business going, instead of blaming it on the economy. I will give them financial security. I will give them not a Mom who looks like she's in pain, but one they know who is working through her pain. I cannot give them this on Christmas day. I will tell them though the best present is yet to come. I can tell them, thank you all for being so special that you not only will get the present you want but the present we all need.

And to Joani, who helped put this book together:

Thank you for all you do to help me; and others going through this nightmare.

~~~~~~~

Chapter 26

My Child

By Karr Marie

You know, that you hurt deeply
You know, that you are confused
You know, that you have chosen to hide from the pain you feel
You know, that each day is a struggle as you try to forget about me.

My hope, is that one day you will come to know ...
that My love, for YOU, never faltered
never wavered.
never failed to grow, with each dawning day
it is ... STILL ... just as it always has been.
STRONG ... just as it always has been.

My hope, is that One day YOU will find ...
the courage and strength
to look at what has always been ... waiting ...
... waiting for YOU to reach out ...
... reach out and feel ...
there is no pain ... here ... only love.

Yes only LOVE ... forever and always ...

~~ Your Mother

This was written by a mother ... but I am certain either parent could feel this way. I am certain that fathers feel the same as mothers. ~~ Karr ~~

~~~~~~~

Chapter 27

Lita Ford's Story

Lita Ford is a rock guitarist and singer, who reportedly has been rejected by her two sons as a result of parental alienation. The video linked below, called *Mother,* speaks to her sons and alludes to the problem of parental alienation. The article is from *USA Today.*

(Photo: Mark Weiss)

Lita Ford's *Mother* has a different kind of Mother's Day message.

The former Runaways guitarist, who also had late '80s solo hits with *Kiss Me Deadly* and *Close My Eyes Forever*, initially intended the song and its video as a message to her two children, from whom she's estranged. But when

Ford saw how her fans in similar circumstances responded to the song after she released it last year on her *Living Like a Runaway* album, she realized how deeply the song spoke to people beyond her own family.

"There was one girl who came up at a meet and greet that we did in California, and she had the lyrics to *Mother* tattooed on her back," says Ford, 53. "Another girl came up and shook my hand, and I said to her, 'Do you have something you want to say to me?' Because she was quiet and looked like she wanted to say something, but I wasn't sure what. She just spilled her guts and started crying. She hadn't seen her son in eight years.

"She cried like a little baby, and I understood her. I understand what it feels like to be the alienated parent."

Parental alienation is "a deep, confusing issue for everybody — the parents, the children," says the mother of two sons, ages 16 and 12. "It's horrific. And there's never really any closure, unlike a death. It's just hanging." While she hopes her sons see the video, she also hopes its message reaches others in similar circumstances and that "it will give them belief and faith and strength to get through whatever it is that they have to go through in order to have their children safe and sane."

The *Mother* video was directed by Victory Tischler-Blue, known in her earlier days as Runaways bassist Vicki Blue. "Vicki and I have been buddies since The Runaways," Ford says. "She was the second main bass player to come into The Runaways. Vicki and I, we've always been tight. She's extremely creative in her way of visual effects, photography and cinematic scenes, and I'm creative musically. We put our creativity together, and we came up with this beautiful piece of footage."

Ford has concerts planned for Australia and Scandinavia this summer, in addition to a U.S. tour. She plans to release a live album recorded last year while touring with Def Leppard and Poison. She says she also has signed with HarperCollins to write her memoir.

Mother

Lyrics and Music by Lita Jones

I am your mother,
Your flesh and blood, your family, yeah
And like no other
Until they bury me 6 foot deep
No matter what the future holds
And even know you just began to grow
Just know you'll always have your mother

The damage is done,
I never wanted things to work out this way
My little ones, how do I say how sorry I am
Some day you'll see the truth
And you'll come running back to me
Just know you'll always have your mother
You'll always have your mother

He lies to you, and
He tries to find
Should be crucified, left to die
He paints an ugly picture of you and I
It's so far from truth
see only when you hurt me
But my love for you
I am your mother
Please understand why I had to leave
Pain was deep,
He was hurting me,
When you look in the sky at a shinning star
Listen to your heart and know who you are
And I'll always be your mother
I'll always be your mother

I'll always be a part of you.

~~~~~~~

Chapter 28

Miranda's Story

By Miranda Rasmussen

My name is Miranda Rasmussen and I have two children ages 10(boy) and 12(girl). Almost four years ago I was in a violent relationship with their father, my husband of six years. One day he hit me and I called the cops and got a restraining order. I made a decision to drop the restraining order and let him move back in about two months later. The abuse got worse and I finally defending myself about six months later hit him to escape. I ended up getting arrested and put in jail. Giving him a tool to use against me.

While I was in jail he filed a restraining order on me and the judge granted it but the kids were not on the order. We had joint custody at the time. Parental alienation began here and we went to several court hearings on divorce issues and child custody issues. There was a case open with children services and closed about four months later. The allegations on the children services reports were made against him. None involved me other than the domestic violence issue I was convicted of. While the cps case was open, he had three separate incidents of physical abuse on my 12 year old.

Meanwhile I was just trying to see them as much as I could and spend as much time as I could with him and stay out of jail. Well he wanted me to sign the house over to him and when I refused he decided to go back to the last custody schedule the courts made, which was only seeing the kids one day a week. Long story short on the above issue, he called my probation officer and had me violated and I ended up going back to jail and getting sentenced and serving some time in jail.

While I was in jail there was several referrals made to cps (the case was closed at the time), which were under investigation. By the time I was released on June of 2011, he had a warrant out for his arrest for a robbery he had committed. He went to jail and CPS put the kids in foster care. When he filed court-restraining order, he put the kids names on and therefore I was technically restrained from my kids. The kids were being physically abused and severely neglected in his care. Once again all they had on me was the restraining order and the fact I was convicted of domestic violence.

So began the process of doing what the court asked to get the kids back. Things were going great while they were in foster care. I didn't have any trouble with children services nor the foster parents. In six months I completed what needed to be completed and was on the road to getting the kids back. I started working and going to school, had my own three-bedroom apartment, kids had their own rooms and everything. Well when I got the kids back for extended periods dad got them back also.

That was when I started seeing some real challenges. My 12 year old freaked out on me saying she did not feel safe and I needed to take her somewhere safe immediately. She wasn't even in trouble when this came out. It came out the blue. Another time she said she loved me but I was manipulating her and controlling her so she didn't want to live with me. The last and final thing she said was she went around telling counselors and her attorney that I threatened suicide if I didn't get custody of them.

The social worker was recommending that the kids stay with me Monday thru Friday and dad on the weekends. Dad disagreed with the recommendation and therefore he filed an objection. By the time we went to the hearing the social worker changed her mind and they all decided that the kids should live with him. And because I was crying and upset, mainly at this social worker who had put my two kids back in the arms of their perpetrator for the fourth time, I told her I was going to request a new worker and that she didn't do her job right. She followed that up with an emergency hearing stating that I was emotionally unstable.

The next hearing took place two weeks later in which the court decided to return the kids to him. We had joint legal custody, he has physical custody and the kids were to be with me every first third and fifth weekend of the month. We were to alternate holidays and four weeks during the summer in two week increments. The court was aware that I might move out of state and if that was the case the order was changed to every other holiday and four solid weeks during the summer. The kids had a right to have a third party present if they felt uncomfortable with me because by that point in court they were saying they didn't want to see me and that they were afraid of me. The judge explained it as a third party like an aunt, uncle or grandparent. The case was at that point closed.

Two weeks went by and it was my weekend for my visit. Since I knew my kids were throwing around these accusations I had decided to try and only take them for a couple hours on Sunday so they didn't feel so uncomfortable. I send their dad a message stating what time I was picking them up and where. I received a message back stating that per court order that I could see them only if I had a cop and supervisor present and that the kids were reading what he was sending to me. Though my daughter had just called me the week prior asking when she was going to see me and I was trying to explain which weekend was my weekend and Dad was in the background trying to convince her I could pick them up that weekend. One thing I learned is I have to obey all orders cause he would go as far as to try and get me for kidnapping.

So within the next two weeks I moved to Memphis, TN. I sent them the remainder of their stuff and a letter explaining that I moved to make a better life for us. I told them my door is always open and that they could call anytime. When they finally got their packages, I got a call from him stating the kids were very mad at me and that I should have scheduled something to say goodbye to them. I was here for a month before I spoke to them again. I sent them a card for thanksgiving and a little package for Halloween and one for winter. I planned on sending them Christmas gifts but I have not got a chance to talk to my daughter about what she wants and her clothing size and all.

I did finally speak with her on the fourth of December. Then, I spoke to my son on the sixteenth but she was sick and so I didn't get a chance to speak to her. Now I have gotten a text stating that his fiancé has the phone at work and the kids are not available to talk. I have called the kids about ten times now and just got the voicemail and now I am getting a message saying the inbox is full.

I have not seen my kids since august 2012 and have not talked to them in twenty days. I am getting ready to give up. It just seems so hard cause I have no clue what to do anymore. I have been patient and I still don't have my kids. I am supposed to have them spring break and it scares me buying the airline tickets and him not even letting them come.

Babies

Even in the wee hours of sleep are my thoughts not restful of my children. To dream about a child you have not seen in over six months. To here an illusion of him calling out your name, saying where are you and I need you? What do I do to pick up the pieces. How do I stay strong and have faith that I am doing the right thing. To hear my kids voice again, I listen to old recordings. That's how I satisfy that urge. But to see my kids again. How to do this I am not sure. Maybe to see some pictures. I don't know where to get pictures from. My heart aches for my children. God knows I want them back in my life. If I lived in California or if I lived in Tennessee the outcome would still be the same. How to move on and leave a child behind? Its not easy to breath sometimes.

I Will Never Stop

I will never stop fighting for my babies until they are returned home safely. Home is with their mother who treats them with kindness and gentleness. She does not ask them to do anything to harm themselves nor others. She will always support their decisions and listen to what ever they may have to say. They shall not fear coming going to her, even if they did not do wrong, because a mother will never judge the actions of their children. I will always love and cherish every moment I have ever had with them and look forward to the awesome memories we will make in the future. I lay my head down at night yet they are always on my mind. I will never stop loving them. They are flesh of my flesh and blood of my blood. I endured nine months to bring them into this world and hour upon hour of excruciating labor. They are my children and I vow to protect them the best I can. I will miss them every day till they are brought home to me. Good night babies, I hope to be able to say that to you soon!

Journaling: December 17, 2012

Looking back at pictures of the kids. I enjoyed my weekly visits with them while they were in foster care. It was so relaxed and I didn't have to worry about getting hurt. I feel I worked so hard to get them back and in the end they didn't come home to me. I don't regret moving to Memphis, this is my life now. This is how I was able to get ahead. This is where I was able to make a fresh start. I cannot let go of the fact I have given birth to two beautiful children. I remember their toddler years as if they were yesterday. I remember when they would hold onto me tightly or I would read to them before bed. We were always doing something fun together. I feel so dead to them now. I talk to them not nearly enough. I have no clue what they look like. The past three years they have grown up without me and now I don't know if I will see them go through the next eight years when they decide what they want to do in life. When they are sick I cannot longer comfort them. When they are having a bad day I cannot longer talk to them. Who am I to these children? What have I done in my life that makes me deserve this kind of life? How do I hold my head up and keep moving forward cause I feel as if I cannot do this any longer? Some days I just feel like I need to end my life. Is that just a cry for help because I don't know how to ask for help or do I truly want to just die and be done with it. I feel so fake as a mother. Does any of this I go through make me less of a mother? I need to live for myself and not my children and I think I have learned that very much so. How come it feels like the only way I will see my kids is if something happens to Brian?

Missing

The phone is ringing and no one is answering. I call and no one decides to answer. How can this be done week after week with no response? How do I find the strength to keep trying over and over again? Its there, I do it even the days I ask myself why. When I wake in the morning, I feel something missing. Its not a whole complete day. I miss them running around the house. My house is so quiet without them here. Some days I don't even know what to do, thinking it would be awesome to go on an adventure with them like the old days. What I would do to have them running around the house, even to just explain to them that we do not run in the house but they can go run outside. I remember listening to sponge bob at five am thinking its way too early to be listening to this darn show. What I would do to have the show on repeat over and over again as long as it meant they were sitting there watching it in a repeat mode. The time is flying so fast, It has already been six months since I have seen them. I feel like I am missing out on priceless memories we could be making together. I just want to make so many happy memories to take away the bad in their life. I want them to be happy and feel loved.

Everything I took for granted. Messy rooms, talking back, nightmares, anything to bring them back. I want them to feel loved. I want to wipe away their tears once again, I want to comfort them and tuck them into bed. I would do anything to have them with me today. I feel like I have lost so much. Bring them home, bring them home, I just want them home!

PAS

Its days like this, everything is so hard on me. I try so hard to survive a day-by-day notion that everything will be alright. But will it? I mean I worked so hard but apparently not as hard as he did at brainwashing the kids. I go day by day not knowing when I will see them again or talk to them again. I put fantasy into believing that I will be able to see them come spring break but like I just put it, Fantasy. The kids conspire against me and I don't even know why. They say such harsh things. I don't know how to deal with this situation. Only say that I did what I thought was best for my children by letting go. But then I get scrutinized over that one too. I hope one day my kids grow up and remember the good times we had when it was the three of us. The times when the true me was there. My daughter tells me, I was changing and she didn't like it. She didn't like me being healthy. Things were different. I can't believe that these kids are so used to the negative environment they went back. They made the choice, yes maybe someone else's prompting but they decided to make accusations against me. Not that I hold it against them but what do I do to combat it. Sometimes sitting back quietly is the best thing to do.

~~~~~~~

Chapter 29

Forty Years and Four Generations of Parental Alienation due to the Failures of the Connecticut Family Court System

By Mike Krukiel

In 1973 my parents were among the first to be divorced under Connecticut's new no-fault divorce laws. I saw plenty of fights between my parents leading up to this time. My father had moved out of the house and had been given the typical "visitation schedule" of Saturday overnight into Sunday every other weekend with my younger sister and myself. I was seven years old and instantly time my father was reduced from him being there everyday to a visitor every other weekend.

My mother began a campaign of denigrating my father and projecting her feelings of hatred for him onto me. I was always grilled by her when returning from visits with my father. I remember she would always make me wait by the door when he would come to pick us up for visitation. She would require him to knock on the door to our house and then watch him from an upstairs window as he got out of his car and approached, to which she would then come downstairs open the door and start an argument often resulting in her denying the visitation time with my father.

Telephone contact with my father between visits was never allowed. If my father did call to talk to us, my mother always intercepted the calls and questioned him, start an argument or just plain hang up and not allow us to ever speak to him. Many times she would bring us with her late at night as she drove around his house, his neighborhood and places he frequented staking him out and spying on him. I was told for years that my father had started another family and had other children that he cared about more than me. Years later I would learn that my father had a vasectomy while still married to my mother and she had signed for the authorization. There was no other family or children and she had lied to me for all those years.

At one point my mother was trying to move us to Florida without my father's consent. I vividly remember being in the forth grade and walking home from school one afternoon and found my father and grandfather waiting for me on the sidewalk. My father talked to me for a while and handed me a paper with his phone number and instructions on how to make a collect call in the event mommy ever moved away. I would later learn that he was trying to prevent the move to Florida in court and had handed me these instruction in case he was unsuccessful.

So much happened during the next five years that by the age of twelve, I had grown so alienated from him that I wouldn't even call him "dad" anymore and instead called him "old man". I didn't care if I saw him again and that's exactly what happened. I know there was legal action still going on between my parents as my father fought for more time with us. But whether it was my mother who ceased allowing me to see him or he gave up the fight all together, the end result was that after twelve years old, I never saw my father again.

My mother had moved us to the city and we were living in a housing project during my teenage years. The absence of a father's influence and involvement in my life amongst a tirade of negative exposure that growing up in a city will bring, was enough to steer me into mischief, drugs, alcohol and failing grades in school. By the time I was in high school, I was lost. If it weren't for two men in my life, my carpentry teacher and my pastor who both helped me turn my life around, my life would have been very different. However, I was still sufficiently alienated from my father and at one point I even wanted to change my last name. My mother constantly questioned me and grilled me, always wanting to know if my father had ever tried to contact me or if I had seen him. It was drilled into me that I was to tell her immediately if he had done so.

The day after I turned eighteen years old, I was alone in the house and the phone rang. I answered it and it was my father. He said, hi Michael, this is your dad. I'd like to talk with you some time". PAS being in full swing by this time, I instinctively said "no way, no way" as I hung up on him and could hear him asking, "why, why" as I was putting the phone down. The call was completely unexpected and shocking at the time, not having heard my father's voice in six years and it would be the last time I would hear my father's voice for many years to come. Years later I would find out that my father had sent cards and tried many times to call me during my teenage years and each time the cards were thrown away and the calls intercepted by my mother.

Years later my father would commit suicide by blowing his head off with a shotgun and thus closing the door for good for any type of reunion. My relationship with my grandfather, who had made a big impact on me as a boy, was also severed and I was not able to meet him or establish a relationship until 1996, when he was almost ninety and with failing health.

The rest of my teens and early twenties were very hard. I look back now and can see how lost I was. Looking for the family life I never had and not having a father's guidance, I married the wrong woman and began the second half of my saga.

I was only married to my first wife Carol for a little over four years, but in this time we had two sons. Michael was born in May of 1993 and Paul was born in September 1994. We were definitely wrong for each other as a couple and there were plenty of problems, but divorce was not on the table........until I was served divorce papers early one

138

morning ordering me out of the house. Not knowing any better at the time, I found an apartment and moved. My sons were nineteen months and five months old. I remember thinking that by the time the divorce was over, I would have been the only one to feel any pain, as my sons would have been too young for any real lasting effects to remain. How wrong I was.

From the very beginning of February 1995, until October of 2010 a fifteen and a half year custody battle would rage on as my son's mother did everything she could to eliminate me from my sons' lives. I sacrificed everything several times over fighting to remain an equal parent with equal rights and equal responsibilities.

For the first five years there were several attempts by my sons mother to move them out of state and out of the country, all of which I fought to prevent. There were countless times I was denied access to my sons as well as any and all information. There were high conflict incidents, false accusations, DCF investigations, court ordered therapy and several Family Relations Custody studies. By 2000, I had exhausted the services that Family Relations could provide and another custody study was ordered with a high profile Psychiatrist after another attempt to move my sons to California. This study took sixteen months and resulted in some expanded, but still not equal access with my sons and more importantly did not sufficiently address the alienation that had been ongoing since 1995 or contain their mother from continuing to do it.

So the incidents, the brainwashing, the denied access and information and direct influencing continued and my son's behavior towards me and their younger half-sister, my daughter with my second wife, grew increasingly worse. The boys would verbally attack their sister and me with accusations that could only have come from their mother. They would write "I hate you" notes and leave them everywhere, be aggressive, disrespectful and self-depreciatory. Their mother told them repeatedly that their sister was not their "real" sister and they believed this, repeated it often and increasingly began to ignore her, hurt her and shut her out. By the spring of 2005 their behavior had reached an all-time high and thus began a sixteen-month period where I did not see them at all. They refused to see me and their mother refused to cooperate with the evaluator who had remained involved since 2000, as well as the attorneys, the AMC or the newly appointed GAL in trying to reunite my sons and me.

This led to a trial at the Regional level, which took place during October of 2006. Seven days of expert witness' and testimony took place. The current orders which had been in place since 2002 were enforced by the judge and I was reunited with my sons and time with them resumed.

In January of 2007, the judge issued her orders from the trial awarding me Sole Legal Custody and Physical Residency based on a "severe state of alienation". This decision made the local newspapers, since a father was awarded custody for something other than for physical abuse or substance abuse. Emotional child abuse was now the subject. The judge also sited my son's mother for being "delusional" and "prone to a distortion of reality" and not having the "psychological makeup" to ensure a healthy bond between my sons and me in this family constellation.

The judge had put in a stipulation in the orders that I was required to move to the town in which my sons had lived with their mother as they had become entrenched in its school system and with their friends. I let my house go and filed for bankruptcy for the second time in ten years and made the move to their town and would rent for the next three years.

Although the judge made the right decision in awarding me custody, she made one very huge mistake and that was granting my sons mother "unlimited verbal contact" along with liberal access and did not put in place any specific orders that would "contain" her from continuing to influence my sons or sabotage or alienate them from me. After the physical transfer took place, their mother immediately bought them cell phones and used them to constantly call and/or instruct them on what to do in my home and accepted their complaints when they would constantly call her. My sons were instructed to write letters of complaints and make constant phone calls to the AMC and the GAL. Within four months their mother had already filed motions for a return of residency to her based on these complaints and false claims of conflict and abuse.

Although these motions were denied, her influencing and alienating continued for almost three years and this caused incredible difficulty in parenting my sons and continuing to repair and grow our relationship. She was relentless in placing her emotions and her irrational and paranoid fears onto the boys and continued to fill their heads with false accusations and her version of a delusional reality. They were made to feel guilty and sorry for mommy for having been "taken away from them" and constantly urged to call the GAL and say they wanted to return living with her.

In June of 2010, the boys relented and agreed to meet with the GAL and express what their mother wanted them to say and their mother immediately filed a motion to have residency returned to her. Although I had Sole Legal Custody and Physical Residency, the GAL agreed to meet with my sons without my knowledge and I was not made aware of what had happened until a marshal arrived at the door to serve me court papers. Essentially their mother took my sons to the GAL behind my back and without my knowledge and the GAL served her purpose by agreeing to meet with the boys and act on what they had been urged to say.

A short reassessment by the original evaluator was ordered by the court and once that was completed, it was concluded that my sons were still alienated, although to a lesser degree, but had almost reached the age of majority and could make the decision for themselves whether they were alienated or not.

After fifteen years of fighting in the courts and not having any more fight left in me, I agreed to the recommendation of my sons returning to their mother. They were seventeen and sixteen years old and there was nothing else I could do and I did not want to put them through any more pain or conflict. Therapy was ordered for my sons, but their mother has refused to take them. I was given a very limited access schedule based on what my sons said they would agree too, however, it turned out that after the orders were put in place and they returned to their mother, they did not want to see me.

It has been a full year now since I last saw my sons. My oldest, who was always the one who had been alienated the most, refuses to call me or respond to my emails. He has graduated high school, to which I was not allowed to attend his graduation ceremony and has gone on to college. My younger son is now seventeen and will respond to a text or email once in a while, but still will not speak to me on the phone. Any and all progress that was made in repairing and restoring our relationship as well as their relationship with their sister during the three years they lived with me has been erased and it looks like there is little hope for the future.

For generations, from my grandfather to my sons, have either been greatly affected or completely destroyed by Parental Alienation.

~~~~~~~

Chapter 30

Empty Spaces

by Mike Quinn

I sit alone here every day,
Thinking of the child you took away.
She was my heart she was my soul.
She was the thing that made me whole.

I have no hope I have no faith, I have no energy,
She was the only pride and joy that rose inside of me,
And now there's just an empty space where laughter used
to dwell.
My heart has got no purpose now, it's just an empty shell.

As I look at children play, in parks and on the beach,
I think about my biggest loss, the child I cannot reach.
Sometimes I wonder what she thinks when her mind
remembers me.
Does she think about the dad she lost, the dad she never
sees.

My days are filled with anger, my nights with painful grief.
How I face each day without her is way beyond belief.
Her toys are strewn about the floor, her bed is empty now.
Abandoned like the autumn leaves shaken from the bough.

There's nothing left for me to have but distant memories,
Of the times we had when she was young and full of
energy.
I hear her voice inside my head calling out to me.
And when I close my eyes to sleep, her face is all I see.

But deep within the darkness that lives inside of me,
There is a tiny glimmer, a spark that's hard to see.
That spark is just a remnant, of the love that is inside

The love which cannot disappear, the love I cannot hide.

I Am Yours To Keep

By Mike Quinn

You are a princess in my heart, and I care for you so much. I love the fondness in you eyes and your tender little touch.

I looked at you when you were born, and knew then straight away, that I would be fore ever here to watch you grow and play.

You bring to me a heart of joy, and memories so great, and a powerful sense of fatherhood that no one can debate.

I watch you sleep and **dream** of things that I can only wonder. That innocent look upon your face just makes my heart grow fonder.

I see you run and jump and shout and calling out my name. No love that I have ever known could ever feel the same. No suffering or tragedy nor deeply seated pain could ever over shadow the bond that we retain.

And so my little princess before you go to sleep, Remember I am your daddy and I am your's to keep.

~~~~~~~

Chapter 31

Pam's Story

By Pam Rapkin Silvestri

My name is Pam. I grew up in NY – in the city, on the Island and upstate. When I was a sophomore and my sister was a junior in high school, our family moved to Oregon to try to patch up my parents' marriage. But it didn't work. My dad left and moved back to NY soon thereafter.

My sister and I were told he had an affair and he didn't love us and he had another whole family. And we didn't see him again. I had been particularly enmeshed with my mom and enjoyed the adult role of her "confidant". She had done an amazing job of teaching me to hate my dad even while they were married, alleging drug abuse, physical abuse and more. I thought my dad was a monster.

Of course I didn't realize that by thinking this about my dad, I would also turn the feeling inward, and begin hating myself. I started a nasty shoplifting habit that put me in jail and I acted out in many other ways including promiscuity, with its attendant issues, and emotional drama. I looked for love in all the wrong places and found all the wrong love. In relationships, I changed to be whatever I needed to be to "keep" the person I was with. I hated myself and adopted an aggressive outlook on life. It wasn't easy to like me.
 Somehow, I got through college and grad school and have a great career. Given my attitude and actions over the years, I have been very lucky and am very grateful for that.

When I went to grad school and got far away from my mom for the first time, I started having thoughts and feelings that I couldn't explain or understand. Looking back, I realize I was beginning to individuate and think and feel for myself.
 I was in NY for grad school, so I checked the phone book

for my dad and he was there. I was still very enmeshed with my mom, but confused. My dad came right into the city to see me. Unfortunately, he tried to defend himself, which just made me defend my mom more. So the relationship didn't grow much at that time, but we kept in touch.

After grad school, at age 25, I moved to Texas for a job and met my husband. I wanted to invite my dad to the wedding. By then I was 30, but still felt the need to get permission from my mom. She was "happily" remarried and wanted my dad to see, so she said yes. But she lost it at the wedding and destroyed the day. She left the reception dramatically, went home and stopped talking to me. That was 1994. I was devastated, but still had all that stuff in my head about my dad, so now I had no parental connections, and was a new bride.

My marriage began to fail early on. My husband had an alcohol issue, but I had no idea how to be a wife. We split after 11 years. By then my mom had apologized (after 7 years of no contact) and I'd jumped right back into a relationship with her, going from nothing right back to enmeshment…no boundaries.

I dated a very young man for four years and took him to meet my mom and dad. Looking at it objectively, and having come from a relatively healthy family, he said he thought maybe I had it backward, maybe my dad was the normal one and my mom was the nut. I still couldn't see it, but finally there was a crack in the facade.

When the young man and I split up (late 2009) I went into clinical depression and was suicidal. I thought it was about the split. A fabulous therapist got me on meds, helped me be able to open up and talk about my FOO issues and at some point, when he felt I was ready to accept and understand what had been done to me and what I had allowed to be done to me and allowed myself to do, asked me if I had heard of PA. He asked me to Google it. That simple suggestion changed my life. We started working through the issues and he helped me parent myself and grow up. That was a process. I had to go through the stages of grief: denial of the situation; anger at my dad, my mom and then myself; some internal bargaining, some leaving and coming back to therapy; deeper depression for a bit; and finally acceptance.

At that point, a friend of mine lost her daughter to kidney failure and she said something at the funeral about making sure your relationships were where they needed to be in case something unplanned happened, so there would be no regrets. I called my dad that day and scheduled a face to face meeting - just us - no wife or boyfriend as buffer. We spent 72 hours together in NYC and I asked him everything I'd always wanted to ask. This time, didn't put my mom down at all. I could clearly see he'd worked to create a life for himself and had moved on from all of that ugliness. He answered all of my questions thoughtfully and honestly, and with evidence. As it turned out most of what my sister and I had been told about our dad was a lie.

The truth was that our mom had a restraining order on our dad so he couldn't see us. He sent letters and they were returned. The kids in his "new" family were his wife's from another marriage. The lies all crumbled in the face of evidence, but I'm glad my dad didn't try to show that evidence to me before I was ready and able to see it. I cannot imagine how hard this has been for him all those years.

My dad's wife was very tentative with me coming back into their lives. I didn't understand at that time, but she had concerns about whether I was still enmeshed with my mom, and whether my dad might be hurt all over again. And since we live in different states and use very different technologies, initial communication was slow and difficult, but it got better with time. Just this year, my dad's wife gave me the gift of more time alone with my dad, and actually told me that she'd felt the need to protect him at first, but has come to understand that my intentions are coming from love. That has been a huge step for us both, in understanding each other's experiences.

My dad and I have been growing closer and closer in the last three years, with at least annual visits. During this last visit, with advice from other alienated parents, and in hopes of deepening my bond with my dad, I asked him if he would share something personal – of his – with me, so that I could have it with me when we're not together. That made a huge impact on him and I could feel more years and walls melt away between us. It was a very special moment for our reconciliation.

I recently purchased an iPad and wi-fi for my dad and connected him with my sister on Facebook. They've not spoken since he left when we were teens. She saw him at my wedding but was not in a place to talk with him.

My mother won't talk to me right now, but I send her loving emails on a regular basis, because it's what I need to do to have no regrets and to be able to sleep at night. My sister is still straddling both relationships. She has three kids who've never met our dad.

My dream is for our entire family to spend time together some day. But many more family members were lost on both sides due to the alienation. I lost very important relationships with my dad's step sisters. They were heroes to me as a kid, especially my Aunt Shelly, because she was who I wanted to be when I grew up. I am most grateful that both of those wonderful women have recently agreed to hear me out and re-establish relationships with me. I never got to meet my Aunt Shelly's husband because they met and then he died while my dad and I were still alienated. My cousins and aunt on my mom's side have also been lost to me, along with their families, because of my enmeshment with my mom. When my mom got angry with them and cut them out of her life, I was seen as a co-conspirator. Most family members don't understand all that has occurred, and many won't talk with me, and some won't talk with my sister. We have lost a lot of years and relationships to PA.

The good news is that in the last three years, as my relationship with my dad has deepened, I have healed so much. I no longer even think about needing a man in my life. I date, but there's no urgency to it at all. And I respect myself enough not to change for anyone, unless it's a change I need to make (and there have been plenty of those as I've learned to parent myself). I'm more confident in all of my relationships, both personally and at work. People like me again. I like me again. My sister and I have gotten closer and we've talked deeply about our history, to try to make sense of it. I am getting better at setting boundaries and at not having resentments. And, my ex-husband and I are best friends. Life is so good.

Update to my story from May 6, 2013
I have to share this. I just got off the phone with my dad and we had one of the most honest and deepest conversations we have ever had. Thanks to all of you, I'm just now starting to understand the depth of what he's been through. I'd written up my story and sent that to him, along with Shelley Jones' daughter's video. My dad was floored. He really didn't understand the depth of what I'd been through either... He knew his side and that he'd lost time with his kids. But he really didn't get how programmed the kids are.

For that reason, he's always been a bit "stiff" around me...and I get it now. He's been worried over the years that I'm still somewhat programmed... and that perhaps I would get re-enmeshed with my mom and whatever he might say could be used against him...again.

He just opened up so much tonight. I'd never known before that my mom's dad was a family court judge and most of her family members were attorneys! My dad was up against a BRICK wall. He said he'd kept much more paperwork and "evidence" than he's shared with me, in case he ever needed it for me or for my sister...but that he decided TODAY...more than 30 years later...to burn all but one letter. He burned nasty mail from my mom. He burned the child support checks he's already shown me. He burned other things he hasn't shown me, but thought he might need someday. And the reason he felt he could do that...finally...is he read my story and saw Heather's video...and he GOT that none of the stuff I've done to him over the years had anything to do with my feelings toward him. He GOT that my sister and I were programmed and programmed very well to hate him. He GOT that I'm done with it and so very much want to be close to him.

But I first reached out to him at 21 and he made a mistake that we both regret now. He tried to defend himself and explain what he thought my mom was doing (of course he had no IDEA of the depth of the damage she'd caused). But just that little effort at defense made my walls go up so far and my defenses of my mom go up so far that we lost more years.

He told me just now that he wishes he'd burned that stuff YEARS ago and just loved me when I so tentatively reached out that first time. He just felt so abused and mistreated. He'd not yet gotten to a place where he could see that he didn't really need to prove anything. I told him I understood.

And I told him I wish I'd been less gullible and malleable as a kid, and had been able to think more for myself, like Heather has. He told me he understood.

We BOTH let fear and shame make our decisions for years...and that wasted SO much time. We both agreed not to have regrets, but to focus on the future and get to know each other as deeply as possible.

I told him how in awe of him I am. And how much I respect him for the path he's traveled. He said "ditto".

So here's the takeaway. Don't lose as many years as we did. Get smart about how you handle this. Don't let fear make your decisions. Make your decisions from LOVE. YOUR KIDS LOVE YOU. THEY ALWAYS HAVE AND THEY ALWAYS WILL. Don't let the AP take MORE of your time from your relationship with your child(ren) by getting you to believe you're not good enough or that you're doing something to deserve this.

I hope my experience will show you that my dad and I came together when we both grew out of needing to blame...and to defend. If I had it to do over again, I would do whatever I needed to do to grow out of the need to blame and defend MUCH sooner...so I could've gotten to the good part much faster. I'm so grateful I'm here now. And I want this crazy experience to help you see what's really happening, and see what you REALLY need to do.

~~~~~~~

Chapter 32

PAS - An Adult Child's Story; The Effects of Parental Alienation

By Anna Jean
Taken From Anna Jean's blog

http://parentalalienationnj.wordpress.com/2011/11/12/an-adult-childs-story-the-effects-of-parental-alienation/

Here I am. The Author of this Blog. Coming through to you from the state of New Jersey. I am passionate about human rights. I am a feminist. I am a wife, a mother of 5, a step-mother of 1, an entrepreneur in the unpaid workforce (although I do hope to get paid for this one day). After many years of caring for my children and struggling to find my "new self" I was slowly led in this direction; becoming a voice for Parental Alienation Awareness and Support.

I have experienced Parental Alienation my entire life. As a child born to parents who couldn't communicate in an emotionally intelligent way, which eventually helped to sever my relationship with my Dad for 11 years, and now as a Step-Mom who has witnessed the slow demise of my Husband's Relationship with his Daughter, which now has been severed for the past 2 years. Here I will focus on my personal experience as a child affected by Parental Alienation.

In order for me to properly describe to you my passion for Parental Alienation Awareness and support allow me to take you back to before I was born, and I'll have to call my family out in order to do this.

It is the late Seventies in New Jersey. My Mom, a woman who runs her own Hypnosis practice along with her Second Husband, meets my Dad, an artistic man who has a bustling Framing business, who is married to his Second

Wife. Well, it may not be all that traditional, but they meet and the rest is, as they say, history, or maybe it's more like the beginning of the future. Fast forward a year or so later I, the author of this Blog, arrive on the Earth a tiny, squirmy, and helpless infant. Reminder: my parents, Hypnosis Lady Mom and Artsy Framer Dad are still married to their Shocked Spouses (I'm putting this together after gathering pieces of information over many years).

Okay now, bear with me, Mom, Dad, and Infant are in the Maternity ward in a New Jersey hospital during the late Seventies and a nurse walks in with the Birth Certificate. Here is where I get a little confused. My original Birth Certificate reads: First Name, Middle Name, Last Name of Mom's Second Husband. What?! What about Last Name of my Dad? Well, according to my Mom, NJ law in the late Seventies requires that a baby born to a married Mom must take Married Mom's last name, which was also Second Husband's last name. **(CORRECTION: AFTER CHECKING OUT MY ORIGINAL BIRTH CERTIFICATE, I REALIZED IT HAS MY MOM'S SECOND HUSBAND LISTED AS: FATHER! MY BIOLOGICAL DAD HAD TO PETITION THE COURT TO REMOVE SECOND HUSBAND'S NAME AS FATHER AND INSERT MY DAD'S!)** It gets really ugly from that point on. Fast forward some time, my Dad, brings the proper Motions in court and has my B.C. and my Last Name changed, which now reflected my Mom's Maiden Name. So, now I don't have Mom's Last Name, nor do I have Dad's Last Name, I don't even have my half-sisters' Last Name (siblings from Mom and First Husband), but I do have Grandma's Last Name. Fine. Or is it?

For the next Seven years of my life my relationship with my Artsy, Framer Dad and his family blossomed. I was loved, I was cherished, I was spoiled with the best clothes. I was fed three meals a day. I was surround by my loving, doting Dad, Aunts and Uncles, Cousins galore. Of course, this was only on visitation weekends because my Dad and my

Mom separated. Since they were never Married, Divorce was never an option. My relationship with my Mom grew as well. We lived with her First Husband from the time I was two years old, and he acted as a perfect Step-Dad to me. I was surrounded by loving Half-Sisters, who I will only refer to as my Sisters here on out because they are my Sisters.

From the age of seven and a half, my relationship was severed with my Dad and his Family. I don't remember much about that. I don't think I even questioned it at that time. I just knew that my Mom said "If you want to have a relationship with your Father you can after you turn 18". Well, for the next 11 years my self-esteem dropped gradually, my confusion rose just the same, my sense of belonging was also displaced. I longed to call someone "Dad". I had a great Step-Dad (Mom's husband #1), but I wanted "Dad".

At the age of 18, not long after my birthday, I received a call from my Step-Mom (Dad's wife #2). Are you sensing any confusion with Step-Mom and Step-Dad? You should. (Figure it out or continue to follow my posts so I can explain further, as that's a story for another day.) My Step-Mom said how long she and my Dad have been waiting to contact me, and would I be interested in meeting him again? My answer was "No". However, I did have a desire to reconnect with my Aunts. I got started on reconnecting after the shock wore off that I was 18 and I was free to do whatever I wanted (not to mention my Mom left me at the age of 17. (Don't worry I lived with my Step-Dad who continued to car for me the best he could.) So, the first beloved Aunt I contacted was unable to talk because she had suffered a severe stroke. Ugh, that was a mighty blow. I cried after I got off the phone because I longed to hear her voice and be embraced in her warm hug once again. My second Aunt that I contacted was so excited, in her anxious way, to hear from me. I felt like a little girl! She invited me to her home, and asked if she could invite

154

my Dad. I said "No". The next week when I came to her home I felt like I was a little girl again; she saved all my photos, my dolls, every toy, my tricycle, my shoes, my clothes. Wow! It was a loving reunion.

Some time after that, I did agree to meet my Dad. I went with my boyfriend at that time, and met my Dad in his Frame Gallery. It was an awkward, but loving meeting. I could immediately feel the hurt in my heart and the longing for all the years lost to return. My tears flooded the room. Why had I blocked off all hurt? Why hadn't I wanted to meet him again? I suppose it was self-protection mode. You know what I cried over the most? The moment the word "Dad" flowed from my lips! I hadn't directed that word at anyone in the 11 years that we were separated!

Meeting my dad again for the first time was a memorable day. Dad played old school videos of me as a child on a felt board screen. He also played me audio recordings of me babbling away as a little girl. He gave me his precious memories that sustained him; his cap and booties from the hospital room the day I was born, the tape measure that was used to measure me the day I was born, a beautifully preserved lock of hair from one of my early haircuts, photos of my bedroom that I never stepped foot into. He always had me in mind and stayed prepared for my return, decorating a bedroom in girl style, buying me a bicycle and wrapping gifts for birthdays and Christmas. My Dad filled this bedroom with these items and would eventually take photos of them when he no longer could afford the two bedroom apartment. He did save a few gifts and all the cards I made for him during my younger years, photos, etc. that I treasure dearly.

Our relationship was awkward, because we lost so many years. However, little by little we became closer, but there just wasn't enough time to make up for the lost years before he died. We had about 6 years reunited before he passed away, only three months after my first son was born. The toughest part for me about our reunification was that I didn't know this family that I had remembered so fondly. My Aunt that had the stroke passed away about two years after I was reunited with my dad, and this was a very traumatic event for me because it was simultaneously a family reunion for me; it was just too much to handle. I am not too close to my remaining blood family on my dad's side, only to my detriment. I am close to my "Step-Mom", who was actually Dad's Wife #2, divorced.

After my dad passed away I inherited all the court documents that he saved regarding custody, name change, and all the ugly court proceedings. It didn't help me when he was alive, and it surely didn't help me after he died, except that I now know he tried to see me, he attempted to be a part of my life. However, that doesn't bring back the years that we lost.

Long after my mom successfully severed my relationship with my dad, long after my dad gave up the fight to see me, long after my dad passed away, and long after my relationship with my mom had settled in to mediocre at best, I am still dealing with the pain, the sadness, the longing of having a loving relationship with both parents.

This would be the end of my story, except now it is happening all over again with my husband and his daughter. In fact, my Husband's entire side of the Family, my Children, and Me...and when she realizes it, my Step-Daughter, The affects Parental Alienation has me revisiting my past and it's preparing the way for my future.

This post about my personal life I hope can help a parent who is naively alienating his or her child from the other parent. I hope at least one person can benefit from reading this, at least one child will be saved from going through a life without both parents.

Expect to hear more from me about what is currently going

on with my dear husband and Step-Daughter and how I am helping others.

Parental Alienation IS Child Abuse. Children need BOTH parents.

~~~~~~~

Chapter 33

My Child
By Stormy Monday

My child, I may not get to be with you
and hold you close and share time with you
all the time...
as we turn the pages in life....but it doesn't mean
I don't want to.
I may not be there, sometimes, when you feel you need
me,
when emptiness surrounds your soul
and the wings of time that help you fly
feel fractured or broken...
but it doesn't mean...
I don't want to.
You have to know and never forget, in those very
moments,
when you feel the most alone, you have to know,
 that I need you, too.
There is never any time, in any night...that passes,
not one second of any day...
that you may feel alone or sad or blue...
not one hour when you're crying..or hurting...
that I'm not crying or hurting
or missing you just as much.
Don't think I'm not hurting inside, just like you.

We're separated by space.
We don't like that we can't be together all the time,
I know this and the miles and hurt feelings
and things said by others that may or may not be true...
will never change the pool of love
we swim through as one...
The pool of love
we share together.
No matter the miles between us or the sadness we feel
inside.
Dear child of mine, I am always with you..inside my heart...
I'm always there.
Inside the vessel of your being, woven with the threads of
both mom and dad,
so carefully wrapped in the blanket of beautiful life
is all the hurt, emptiness and confusion that I want so much
to take away from you and throw into the far-off enigma...
and give to you a place, alive with all the love we both feel,
inside,
for you.
There is a deep, deep cavern, where your dreams swim
inside me and they never leave.
Sometimes I feel you leave that place,
that refuge of warmth
filled with all the love we share
and I reach for you, in my heart, and I'm frightened
you're slipping into the thoughts of others
and drifting into a distant abyss, drifting from who you and

I,

both know we are,

together. My child, dear child of mine...

I love you. More than the profound depth of

the poets honey-soaked and silky syllables ...

and higher than the flight of the captivating

American Eagle...

soaring through an endless sky...

far deeper than the eyes of a hopeless romantic...

I love you...

When your heart soars through the wonders of the

Heavens on high

and the happiest and best smile you ever smiled...

dances inside the beauty of your eyes...

No other life could ever matter more...to me.

My child...

I love you.

(C) Stormy Monday

I Got This

By Stormy Lee Monday

One day I was looking for myself. I realized I'd broken into a million pieces, somewhere along the way. I was very hard to find, for I was everywhere and yet, I was nowhere. I tried desperately to put me back together, but, the fragments of my soul were tiny pieces that I couldn't find. All over the place I laid. I was a mess and in my confusion, I became very lost. "What do I do", I asked myself, but, I just couldn't find any answers. For many years, I stumbled about leaving pieces of my soul, all over. As time passed, less and less of me, were who people came to know. Through the years, I became a broken shadow of who I was put in this World to be. One day, a disheveled, homeless man wearing an old, torn black shirt, whose face, was filled with the scars of weary time, stopped me, as I walked along the road. His gaze pulled me into a Native smile with a crooked mouth filled with broken teeth. As I looked past the broken teeth and into his deep, searching eyes, his voice grabbed me and held me. "Listen to me," he said, "You are lost. But, in losing yourself, have you not really found the better you. The man inside you, that could not find the way, he left...so, you could be here." He had an old hat in front of him with a few crumpled dollars in the bottom. I had 7 dollars in my pocket. It was my belief he could use 5 of those dollars, more wisely than me. So, without another thought, I dropped the five in his hat. He nodded in approval and with his kind and thoughtful way, whispered, "thank you." I thought about what he said as he sat back against the wall. Before the thank you. The cardboard under him was well-used and I knew he had been here before. "So, what does that mean?" I ask him. "You know, what you said before..what does that mean?" "It means, my friend, we are lost, really. All of us. But, in our best or worse days, how you treat the man who has nothing... is who you really are. So, from where I'm sitting and I'm okay with where I am, by the way...my friend, you are not lost at all. You are rich in spirit and blessed beyond all understanding to many...just know, you will grow beyond your years and spread your wisdom and love...all across the land." Time and people will grow to realize you have a higher purpose in this World. You have many great things of value to share and people from everywhere will someday learn many things from you. What you have to offer this World is important in the bigger and more important picture." "Hmmmm, from this homeless man, in this short time, with these few words, I had learned so much, about me. I had learned things that made sense to me. Things I would learn to apply in my life and grow into a much better man in this world. I looked inside his eyes and stood up, nodding my head with love for this man...then I walked away. I felt renewed inside my spirit. I felt like a new man that had been born all over again. My inner strength had grown, suddenly, and I felt so alive. As I walked from the wrinkled old man, I turned to thank him one more time. He was gone. He wasn't there. Once, when I was a little boy, my daddy told me, son, always be good to everyone. You never know when Jesus might pretend to be a homeless man. Treat every man with that, inside your thinking, and you will grow rich, in the ways of life. That is the better place for wealth. My mind flashed back to my daddy's wise and meaningful words.Time passed and turned into years...As I walked on down the road, I found myself. I put me back together. With each passing moment, I found all the broken pieces that had crumbled into the soil. Somehow, with the help of the Great Spirit, a homeless man and countless life lessons along the way, I found a new belief in myself. Who I was, became the most of all I am... and in doing so, I was whole again. I became ME. The real me. Not the dope-head, the player or the street-hustler, but, the Artist, the author, the Poet and on and on... My heart cried with the joy of ten thousand men, for, I loved the new spirit that now lived, beautifully, within my heart. Years later, I was about to do a show in Austin, Texas. I was performing poetry set to music, from my recently released book, "The Secret Path". On my way out onto the stage, I stopped, abruptly, to look in a mirror to check my hair and make sure I looked okay. When I looked inside the mirror, time froze, for just a moment. A weary, old man, wearing a torn black shirt, with an old hat on, was looking back at me. He was smiling, through those broken teeth and wrinkled gaze, just looking right at me. The beautiful memory of that old man, so many years ago, flooded my mind and came rushing back to me. He said to me, "You got this." I stood there, just smiling right back at him, thinking of all the things I'd been through and the long road I'd traveled, since we'd first met."Yes...I do. I got this!"He nodded at me and his crooked smile faded into the mist and disappeared inside the mirror. That show and many more, have been so successful. Yes, I feel blessed and I feel grateful. But, the road has been long and not always easy. Ya know, inner-strength, confidence and belief in yourself, comes from many places. In your youth and along the way, many will try to knock you down and tear away the fabric of who you really are. Sometimes, it won't be easy. Sometimes, your World will change in the blink of an eye, beyond your control. You may lose a loved one that meant the entire World to you. You may lose a child more precious to you than life itself, in a custody battle. You may suffer beyond your own understanding, when someone you deeply love, walks out the door. There are so many things in life that will stop you in your tracks and make you question your own self-worth. I'm telling you, it will be hard as hell, but, work through the pain and suffering. Give yourself time to process the hurt and the sorrow. Time really is a healer. Maybe decisions about your life don't unravel the way you'd hope'd for. Step back and breathe. Refocus your energy. Cry if you have to. But, in time and ultimately, get your ass up and walk through all those life lessons. Walk through everything trying to stop, what you believe. Dream for you and live for what feels right for you. No one can stop your dream, but you. Always remember, we all have to grieve sometimes. That's the way life works. Do what the voice inside your head makes you understand. I'm here to tell you with all the fiber of my being... no matter what..remember this. Anytime, you have a moment in life, when you feel the walls coming down or you feel the World isn't fair or people don't act right. My friend, none of us act right, sometimes. We're all imperfect humans with our arms out-stretched for a life-line. Well, whatever happens in your life that seems to be the most incredible obstacle that could ever possibly be in your way, something you feel you just can't get through. First and foremost, never lose your faith in the Great Spirit...then, you reach deep inside yourself... you just stop what you're doing right now and reach inside yourself. Just stop what you're doing and breathe in a long, steady breath. Now,

you just look in that mirror, look right inside your own eyes
and you tell yourself..."I got this!"
(c) Written by Stormy Lee Monday

~~~~~~~

Author Resource Listing

Thank You

Thank you for purchasing this eBook. Parental Alienation Syndrome is domestic violence and abuse. If you are or know of someone who is a victim of PAS, please go to these links for help and support, or tell someone else about this book. Donate to our cause or other causes educating victims, Courts, Judges, GALs, Therapists, and other professionals involved and advocating the end of Parental Alienation Syndrome. Every positive action creates a positive impact.

About the Contributors & Resources

The people who have contributed their stories and poems are presented in alphabetical order by first name. Some have chosen to omit biographies, photos, or use their full names in order to protect their privacy.

PAS Resources:

www.pas-intervention.com

PAS Yahoo Support Group Links

PAS Intervention on Facebook

PAS Guardian Angels and Second Wives Club Facebook

"Where Did I Go Wrong? How Did I Miss the Signs?
Dealing with Hostile Parenting & Parental Alienation"

by Joan T. Kloth-Zanard

~~~~~~~

PAS Intervention is a Federally Tax Exempt Charitable organization approved for tax-deductible contributions under Sec. e501(c)(3) of the Internal Revenue Service

166

57778120R00109

Made in the USA
Lexington, KY
26 November 2016